PILLOWS WITH *Personality*

Introduction

Have you ever looked for just the right pillow to fit in with your decor, but nothing was quite right? The fabric wasn't the right color, the trims were not appealing or the style wasn't what you had in mind.

As you look through this book of 77 different patchwork pillows, you are bound to find pillows to accent any room in your home. There are fifteen groupings of pillows shown, but you can mix and match any of the blocks using your own fabrics and trims. The possibilities are endless. You can even use the blocks to make a matching quilt for your bedroom, a lap quilt for your den or a wall hanging for the living room.

There are complete instructions for each pillow as shown, but you can add fringe where we have added a ruffle, or beading where we have cording. You can make your pillows to your own specifications using the Pillow Instructions on pages 12 to 15 as a guide.

You will find that you can't stop at just one. You will end up making pillows for everyone on your gift list or for every room in your home!

Editor	Bobbie Matela
Art Director	Brad Snow
Publishing Services Manager	Brenda Gallmeyer
Managing Editor	Linda Causee
Assistant Art Director	Karen Allen
Copy Supervisor	Michelle Beck
Copy Editors	Conor Allen, Nicki Lehman
Technical Editors	Chad Summers, Christina Wilson
Photography	Tammy Cromer-Campbell
Photography Assistant	Josh Cromer
Graphic Arts Supervisor	Ronda Bechinski
Graphic Artists	Erin Augsburger, Joanne Gonzalez
Chief Executive Officer	John Robinson
Publishing Director	David J. McKee
Book Marketing Director	Craig Scott
Editorial Director	Vivian Rothe

Photography locations:
Terry's Furniture of Longview, Texas;
Hank's Furniture of Longview, Texas.

Pillows were made by Jackie Breitenfeld, Linda Causee, Cheryl Gould, Anne Hogan, Sandy Hunter, Claire Jungerson, Sue Klinker, Robin Radovich, Sue Ragan and Christina Wilson.

Thank you to the following companies who generously supplied products for our quilts:

Bernina® of America: Artista 180 sewing machine

Güterman: 100% cotton sewing thread

Northcott Silk, Inc.: fabrics
http://www.northcott.net/

Fairfield Processing Company: pillow forms
http://www.poly-fil.com/index.asp

Therm-O-Web HeatnBond:
paper-backed fusible web
http://www.thermoweb.com/consumer.html

Wrights: cording, ruffles and ribbons
http://www.wrights.com/

Mill Hill: beads

American School of Needlework®
excellence in instruction

DRG Publishing
306 East Parr Road
Berne, IN 46711
©2004 American School of Needlework
TOLL-FREE ORDER LINE or to request a free catalog (800) 582-6643
Customer Service (800) 282-6643, Fax (800) 882-6643

Visit AnniesAttic.com.

Customer Service (800) 282-6643, **fax** (800) 882-6643

Contents

General Directions

The Fabric

Choose fabric for your pillows that is 100 percent cotton fabric. It is easy to work with and will wear much better than almost any other type of fabric.

Prewashing is not necessary, but pretesting your fabric for colorfastness and shrinkage is strongly advised if you plan to wash your pillows. Start by cutting 2"-wide strips from each fabric that you will be using. To determine whether the fabric is colorfast, immerse each strip separately into a clean bowl of extremely hot water, or hold the fabric strip under hot running water. If your fabric bleeds a great deal, all is not lost. You might be able to wash all of that fabric until all of the excess dye has washed out. Fabrics that continue to bleed after they have been washed several times should be eliminated.

To test for shrinkage, take each saturated strip and iron it dry with a hot iron, being careful not to stretch it. When the strip is completely dry, measure and compare it to your original 2"-wide strip. If all your fabric strips shrink about the same amount, then you really have no problem. If you wash your finished pillow, you may achieve the puckered look of an antique quilt. If you do not want this look, you will have to wash and dry all of the fabric before beginning so that shrinkage is no longer a problem. Use spray starch or sizing when ironing fabric to give a crisp finish.

Techniques

Rotary Cutting

Supplies

For rotary cutting, you will need a mat, acrylic ruler and a rotary cutter. There are many different brands and types of supplies on the market. Choose supplies that are comfortable for you.

Mats come in various sizes, but if you are new to rotary cutting, an 18" x 24" mat is a good choice. Be sure to keep your mat on a flat surface when not in use so that it doesn't bend. Also, avoid direct sunlight—heat will cause the mat to become warped. Bent or warped mats will decrease the accuracy of your cutting.

Acrylic rulers are a must for safe and accurate cutting. Be sure your ruler has accurate ⅛" increment markings in both directions as well as a 45-degree marking. Either the 6" x 24" or 6" x 12" size is recommended. The larger size is long enough to use with the fabric only folded once. Using the smaller size requires that you fold the fabric twice in order to cut.

There are several different rotary cutters currently available. Read the labels to find one with features that you prefer, such as type of handle, adaptability (for right- and left-handed use), safety, size and cost.

Cutting Strips

Iron fabric to remove wrinkles, then fold in half lengthwise, bringing selvages together. Fold in half again, **Fig 1**. Be sure there aren't any wrinkles in the fabric.

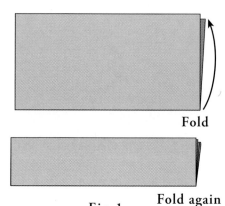

Fold

Fold again

Fig 1

Square up fabric first. Place folded fabric on cutting mat with the fabric length on the right (or left for left-handers), **Fig 2**. Line up fold of fabric along one of the

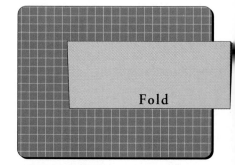

Fold

Right-handed

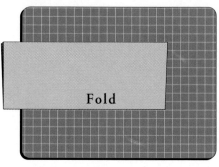

Fold

Left-handed

Fig 2

mat grid lines. Place acrylic ruler near cut edge, with ruler markings even with mat grid. Hold ruler firmly with left hand (right hand for left-handers), with small finger off the mat to provide extra stability. Hold rotary cutter with blade against ruler and cut away from you in one motion, **Fig 3**.

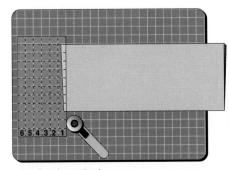

Right-handed

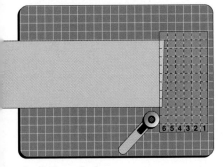

Left-handed

Fig 3

Place ruler with appropriate width line along cut edge of fabric and cut strip, **Fig 4**. Continue cutting the number of strips needed for your project.

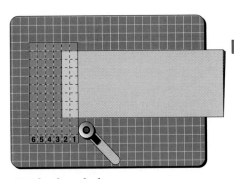

Right-handed

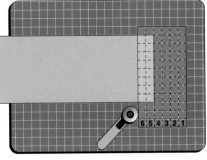

Left-handed

Fig 4

Note: *After cutting a few strips, check to make sure your fabric is squared up and re-square if necessary. If you don't, your strips may have a "V" in the center, **Fig 5**, causing inaccurate piecing.*

Fig 5

Cutting Squares

Place a stack of strips (no more than four) on cutting mat; be sure strips are lined up evenly. Cut required number of squares or rectangles referring to the project instructions, **Fig 6**.

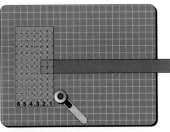

Right-handed

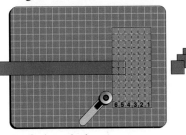

Left-handed

Fig 6

Half-Square Triangles

Some of the pillow blocks require half-square triangles. Half-square triangles have their short sides on the straight grain of the fabric. This is necessary if these edges are on the outer edge of the block.

There are two ways to cut and sew half-square triangles. First, cut squares the required size, then cut in half diagonally, **Fig 7**. Sew triangles together to form a square, **Fig 8**.

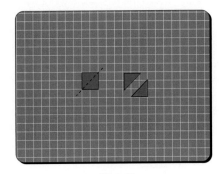

Fig 7

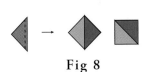

Fig 8

Second, cut squares the required size. Place two squares right sides together. Draw a diagonal line from corner to corner on wrong side of lighter square, **Fig 9**.

Fig 9

Sew ¼" from each side of diagonal line, **Fig 10**.

Fig 10

Cut along drawn line to get two squares, **Fig 11**; press open.

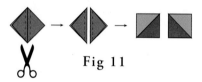

Fig 11

The second method is especially useful when many of the same triangle squares are needed for your project.

Quarter-Square Triangles

Quarter-square triangles are made by cutting a square, then cutting the square diagonally into quarters, **Fig 12**. These triangles have their longest side on the straight grain of the fabric.

Fig 12

Stitch & Flip

The stitch-and-flip method of sewing is used for many of the pillows in this book. For stitch and flip, instead of cutting triangles and octagons, you will cut and sew squares (or rectangles) together. This time-saving method is easier than sewing two bias edges together.

Place small square in corner of larger square (or rectangle) with right sides together. Sew diagonally from corner to corner of small square, **Fig 13**.

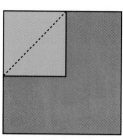

Fig 13

*Hint: If you are uncomfortable sewing diagonally, draw a line from corner to corner on the wrong side of the smaller square with a pencil or removable fabric pen, **Fig 14.***

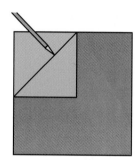

Fig 14

Trim corner about ¼" from seam line; flip triangle open and press, **Fig 15**.

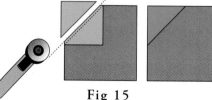

Fig 15

Repeat at opposite corner to finish, **Fig 16**.

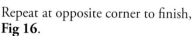

Fig 16

Hint: Save resulting triangles for a future project.

Curved Piecing

Curved piecing uses two pattern shapes, one with an inner curve and one with an outer curve.

Make templates by tracing pattern onto template plastic. ***Hint:*** *If you prefer, make a cardboard template by tracing pattern onto tracing paper. Glue or tape paper to cardboard, then cut out template. Be sure to include all markings on template.*

Trace template onto wrong side of fabric, including all markings, **Fig 17**. Cut out pieces along drawn lines.

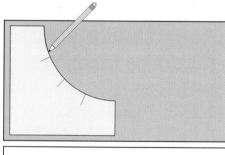

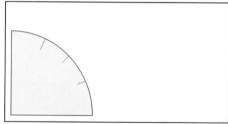

Fig 17

Place two pieces right sides together matching center marks on curved edges, **Fig 18**. ***Note:*** *Keep piece with inner curve on top throughout.*

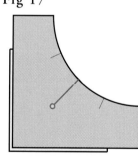

Fig 18

Match outer two marks and pin, **Fig 19**.

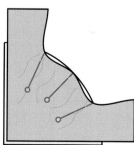

Fig 19

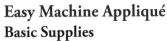

Pin at edges of curve, **Fig 20**.

Sew along curved edge using ¼" seam allowance, **Fig 21**.

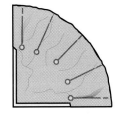

Fig 20

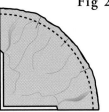

Fig 21

Press seams toward outer edge, **Fig 22**.

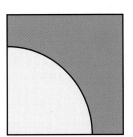

Fig 22

Chain Piecing

For faster and more efficient sewing, use chain piecing when there are several of the same shapes to sew. For example, if you have several triangles to sew together, place two triangles right sides together; sew along longest edge, **Fig 23**. Without lifting the presser foot or cutting the thread, sew next pair. Continue sewing pairs of triangles until all are sewn, **Fig 24**. Press seams toward darker fabric. Pairs can be cut apart when needed.

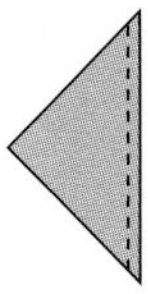

Fig 23

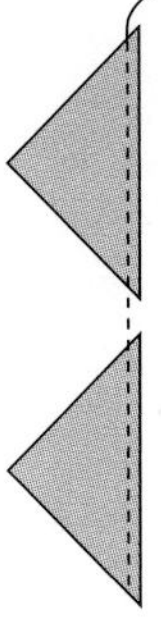

Fig 24

Easy Machine Appliqué
Basic Supplies

Paper-Backed Fusible Web – Use this to trace patterns and fuse appliqué pieces onto background fabric. Since some paper-backed fusible webs are thicker than others, be sure to look at manufacturer's label to be sure that you can sew through it easily without gumming up the needle.

Invisible monofilament thread – Use invisible thread to machine-stitch along edges of appliqué pieces, if desired.

Basic Technique

Trace number of pattern pieces needed onto paper side of fusible web. Rough-cut around pieces. *Note: If you are making several pieces that will use the same fabric, trace those patterns together, Fig 25. This will save cutting time.*

Fig 25

Place traced pieces onto wrong side of appropriate fabric; iron in place to fuse following manufacturer's directions. Cut out pieces along drawn lines. Note that the finished blocks will be a mirror image to the original patterns.

Hint: To eliminate stiffness from fusible web, cut out center of design leaving about ¼" of paper-backed fusible web along outside edge of pattern. Fuse to wrong side of fabric and cut out along outside edge of pattern.

Cut background fabric about 2" larger in both directions than finished size.

Referring to quilt photo, position pieces on background fabric. Fuse in place following manufacturer's directions.

To finish edges (if desired), use invisible monofilament thread in your machine and a neutral thread in the bobbin to machine-zigzag along raw edges of all appliqué pieces, **Fig 26**. *Note: Use a short stitch length and width.*

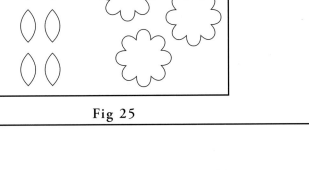

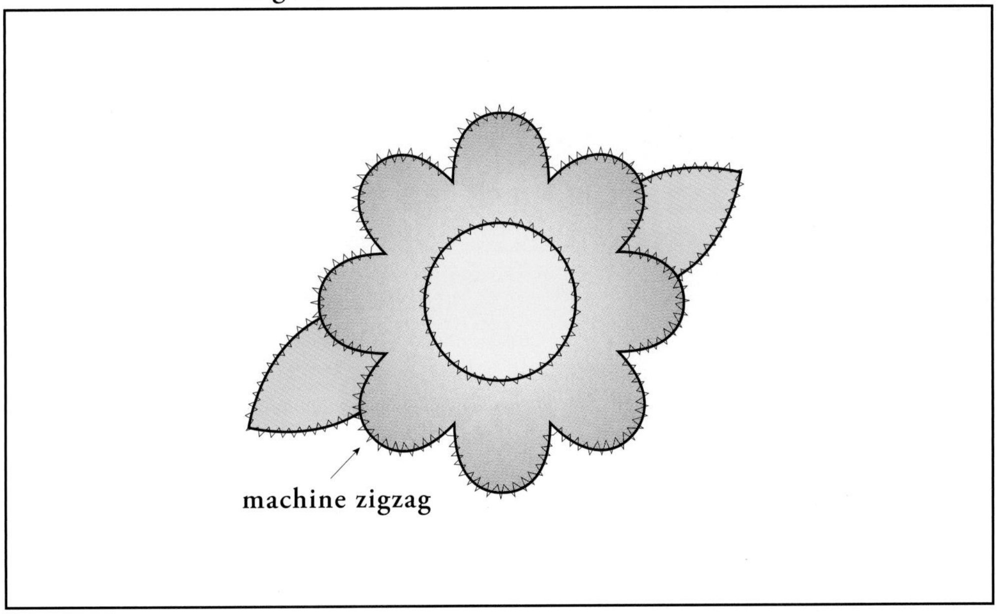

machine zigzag

Fig 26

Foundation Piecing

The Patterns

Some of the pillows are made using foundation-pieced blocks. The patterns are in full color and some have more than one section that must be foundation-pieced individually, and then sewn together. Bold lines that are also the cutting lines indicate these sections. A piecing diagram is included with each block showing the piecing order of the sections.

Also included with each block pattern is a photograph showing the completed block. Note the finished blocks are mirror images of the original patterns, **Fig 27**.

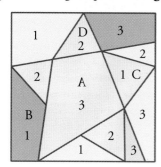

Pattern

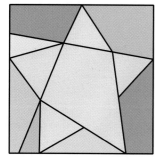

Finished Block

Fig 27

Foundation Material

Before sewing, decide the type of foundation on which to piece your blocks. There are several options. Paper is a popular choice for machine piecing because it is readily available and inexpensive. Copier paper works well, but newsprint found in office supply stores is much easier to handle since it is not as stiff. The paper is removed after the blocks are completely sewn.

Another alternative for foundation piecing is muslin or cotton fabric that is light-colored and lightweight for easy tracing. The fabric will add another layer that you will have to quilt through, but that is only a consideration if you are going to hand-quilt. Also, if you use a fabric foundation, you will be able to hand-piece your blocks if that is your desire.

A third option for foundation material is Tear Away or Fun-dation translucent non-woven material. Like muslin, it is light enough to see through for tracing, but like paper, it can be easily removed before quilting.

A new type of "disappearing" foundation material by W.H. Collins is called WashAway foundation paper. After sewing, place block in water and the foundation dissolves in 10 seconds.

Preparing the Foundation

Trace the block pattern carefully onto foundation material. Use a ruler and a fine-point permanent marker or fine-line mechanical pencil to make straight lines; be sure to include all numbers and letters for multiple sections.

Cutting the Fabric

One of the biggest advantages to foundation piecing is that you do not have to cut exact pieces for every block. This is especially important for smaller blocks or blocks with many small pieces. It is much easier to handle a small section or strip of fabric than it is to handle a triangle where the finished size of the sides is ¼".

The main consideration for using fabric pieces for a particular space is that the fabric must be at least ¼" larger on all sides than the space it is to cover. Squares and strips are easy to figure, but triangle shapes can be a little tricky to piece. Use generous-sized fabric pieces and be careful when positioning the pieces onto the foundation. You do waste some fabric this way, but the time it saves in cutting will be worth it in the end.

*Hint: Measure the width of a particular space on your pattern; add ½" and cut a strip to that width, **Fig 28**. You will save time since you won't have to trim each seam allowance as you go.*

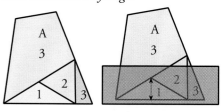

Fig 28

How to Make a Foundation-Pieced Block

1. Prepare foundations as described previously in Preparing the Foundation. If the foundation pattern has more than one section, such as Crazy Star on page 24, cut apart along the bold lines to separate pattern into smaller sections, **Fig 29**.

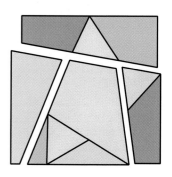

Fig 29

2. Turn foundation section with un-marked side facing you and position piece 1 right side up over the space marked "1" on the foundation. Hold foundation up to a light source to make sure that fabric overlaps at least ¼" on all sides of space 1, **Fig 30**. Pin or use a glue stick to hold fabric in place.

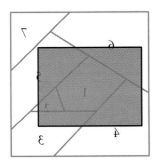

Fig 30

Hint: *Use only a small amount of a fresh glue stick to hold fabric in place. It is especially helpful to use a glue stick to keep larger or narrow pieces in place on the foundation until the blocks are sewn together.*

3. Turn foundation over. With marked side of foundation facing you, fold foundation forward along line between spaces 1 and 2 and trim fabric about ¼" from fold if needed, **Fig 31**.

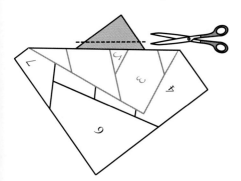

Fig 31

4. Place fabric piece 2 right sides together with piece 1; edge of fabric 2 should be even with just-trimmed edge of fabric 1, **Fig 32**.

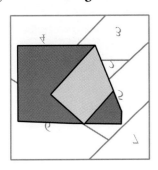

Fig 32

Double-check to see if fabric piece chosen will cover space 2 completely by folding over along line between spaces 1 and 2, **Fig 33**.

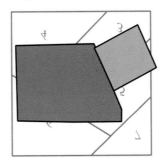

Fig 33

5. With marked side of foundation facing you, place on sewing machine, holding fabric pieces together. Sew along line between spaces 1 and 2 using a very small stitch (18–20 stitches per inch), **Fig 34**. Begin and end sewing two to three stitches beyond line. You do not need to backstitch.

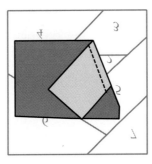

Fig 34

Hint: *Sewing with a very tiny stitch will allow for easier paper removal later. If paper falls apart after stitching, your stitch length is too small and you will need to lengthen the stitch slightly.*

6. Turn foundation over. Open piece 2 and finger-press seam, **Fig 35**. Use a pin or dab of glue stick to hold piece in place if necessary.

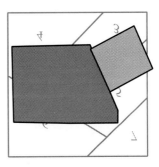

Fig 35

Hint: *If using strips, trim extra length being sure to leave enough to cover entire area plus seam allowance.*

7. Turn foundation with marked side of foundation facing you; fold foundation forward along line between spaces 1, 2 and 3 and trim ¼" from fold if necessary, **Fig 36**. *Note: If you have used a premeasured strip as described in Cutting the Fabric, you will not need to do this step.*

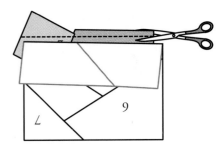

Fig 36

8. Place fabric 3 right side down, even with just-trimmed edge, **Fig 37**.

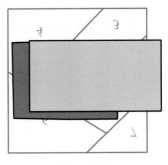

Fig 37

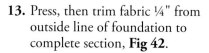

9. Turn foundation to marked side and sew along line between spaces 1, 2 and 3; begin and end sewing two to three stitches beyond line, **Fig 38**.

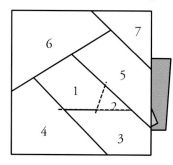

Fig 38

10. Turn foundation over, open piece 3 and finger-press seam. Glue or pin in place, **Fig 39**.

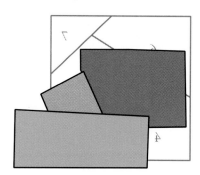

Fig 39

11. Turn foundation with marked side facing you. Fold foundation forward along line between spaces 1, 3 and 4; trim to about ¼" from fold, **Fig 40**.

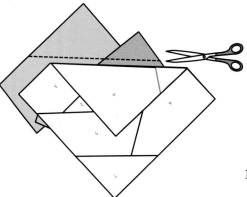

Fig 40

Hint: *If using a paper foundation, carefully pull paper away from stitching for easier trimming. If using a fabric foundation, fold it forward as far as it will go and trim.*

12. Continue trimming and sewing pieces in numerical order until section is complete, **Fig 41**. Make sure pieces along the outer edge are large enough to allow for the ¼" seam allowance.

13. Press, then trim fabric ¼" from outside line of foundation to complete section, **Fig 42**.

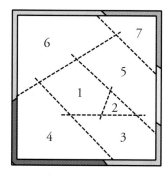

Fig 42

14. Complete remaining sections of block in same manner.

15. If your block has more than one section to piece (see Crazy Star, page 24), refer to piecing diagram shown with each block pattern. To sew sections, place first two sections right sides together; push a pin through corner of top section going through to corner of bottom section. Check to be sure pin goes through both corners and is perpendicular (going straight up) to section, **Fig 43**. If not, pin again until corners match.

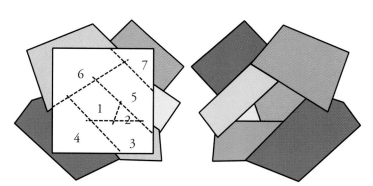

Fig 41

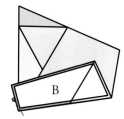

Fig 43

Repeat at opposite end of seam line to match corners, **Fig 44**. It is also a good idea to pin the intersections of seams that should line up between the two sections.

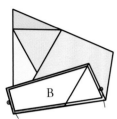

Fig 44

Hint: *If desired, baste sections together by hand or machine. Check sections again; if everything matches up, sew together with regular stitches. Basting takes a little time, but the extra effort will be worth it in the end.*

16. Once pieces are lined up correctly, sew along edge of foundation using a regular stitch length, **Fig 45**.

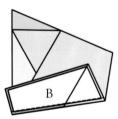

Fig 45

17. Sew remaining sections together, referring to the order in the piecing diagram with each pattern.

Hint: *Do not remove paper yet. It is better to remove paper after blocks have been sewn together. Since grain line was not considered in piecing, outer edges may be on the bias and, therefore, stretchy. Keeping paper in place until after sewing will prevent the blocks from becoming distorted. Stay stitching along outer edge of block, Fig 46, will also help keep fabric from stretching out of shape.*

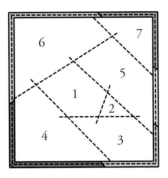

Fig 46

Highlights and Hints for Foundation Piecing

• Begin and end sewing at least two to three stitches beyond line you are sewing on, **Fig 47**.

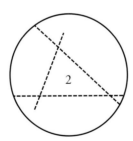

Fig 47

• Don't worry if your stitching goes through a whole space and into another space, **Fig 48**; it will not interfere with adding subsequent pieces.

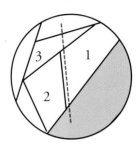

Fig 48

• Finger-press or press with an iron after every seam. The little wooden "irons" found in quilt shops or catalogs work great.

• Use a short stitch, around 20 stitches per inch.

• Trim seam allowances to ⅛"–¼" (or smaller if necessary for small sections).

• Don't worry too much about grain line. Sewing to a foundation stabilizes the fabric and will prevent it from getting out of shape.

• When sewing spaces with points, it is easier to start sewing from the wide end towards the point, **Fig 49**.

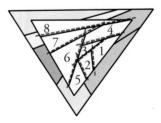

Fig 49

• Directional prints are not recommended unless they are used only once in a block or are placed where they can be used easily in a consistent manner. If directional prints are placed randomly, the effect in the finished block may be undesirable.

Making a Pillow

Basic Pillow

Once you have pieced your block(s) for the pillow top, stay-stitch a scant ¼" from all four edges.

Cut backing fabric the same size as your pillow top. Place pillow top and backing right sides together. Begin sewing along one side away from corner using a ¼" seam allowance, **Fig 1**. *Hint: Backstitch at the beginning and end of sewing around pillow. This will prevent seam from coming apart when turning and placing pillow form in pillow.* At corners, sew in a gentle curve rather than pivoting around the needle, **Fig 2**. Continue sewing until you are about 10" from the start to leave an opening for turning, **Fig 3**. *Note: The 10" opening is adequate for the 12" and 14" sizes. Increase to 12" for the 16" size and 24" for the large 30" floor pillow.*

Fig 1

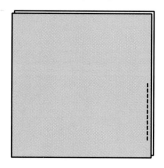

Fig 2

Fig 3

Clip corners, turn pillow right side out and place pillow form through opening. Whipstitch opening closed, **Fig 4**.

Fig 4

Hint: If pillow form is not full enough to fill corners of pillow, add a little polyester fiberfill if desired.

Pillows With Trimmed Edges

There are several different types of trim that can be used to enhance your pillow—cording, fringe, beads and braid to name a few. The trims used for the pillows in this book are sewn into the seam as the pillow front and back are sewn together.

Place trim along outer edge of right side of pillow top with the lip of the trim even with the raw edge of pillow, **Fig 5**. Clip corners of trim so it lays flat, **Fig 6**.

Overlap ends of trim about ½" and turn into seam allowance.

Fig 5

Fig 6

Hint: Use a small amount of Fray Check at clippings and ends of trim to prevent raveling.

Using a long straight stitch, baste trim to pillow top along all four sides, **Fig 7**.

Fig 7

Place top and backing right sides together. Starting on one side away from corner, begin sewing along basting stitches. As you approach a corner, begin sewing in a gentle curve rather than pivoting at the corner, **Fig 8**. This will prevent pointy corners. Leave a 10"–12" opening for turning.

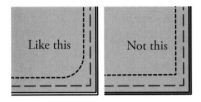

Fig 8

Turn pillow right side out through opening, Place pillow form through opening, then whipstitch opening closed.

Hints for cording and thick trims: *Use a zipper foot so that stitching can be as close as possible to the cord,* ***Fig 9.*** *Gently curve trim at corners.*

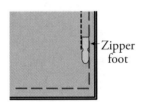

Fig 9

Hints for beaded trims: *To keep beads out of the way while sewing, tape beads to pillow front prior to sewing.*

Optional: *Trims such as cording or braid can be added by hand to pillow edges after the pillow is completed. Use matching thread and blind stitches.*

Pillows With a Flange Edge

Make block for pillow front; sew strips for flange to opposite sides, then to remaining two sides. Press seams toward flange.

Cut backing the same size as pillow front.

Place pillow front right sides together with backing. Sew along all four edges using a ¼" seam allowance, pivoting at corners and leaving a 10"–12" opening for turning. Turn pillow right side out through opening. Press pillow flat.

To make flange edge, machine-stitch in seam between flange strips and pillow, beginning on same side of opening at edge. Gently curve at corners and leave a 10"–12" opening for turning that is parallel (even) to opening in outer edge, **Fig 10**.

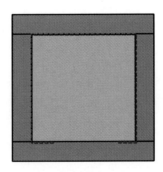

Opening

Fig 10

Place pillow form through both openings. Using a zipper foot, finish sewing in seam between flange and pillow top. **Hint:** *Try to push pillow form away from the opening that is to be stitched to make sewing easier.*

Whipstitch outer opening closed.

Pillows With a Flap

Some of the pillows have flaps that are triangular as well as rectangular. Some are patchwork and some are pieces of fabric.

Cut or piece the flap front according to individual pattern instructions. Cut another piece of fabric the same size for flap backing.

Place flap front right sides together with pillow backing. Sew using a ¼" seam allowance, **Fig 11**. Press triangle open with seam allowance toward backing.

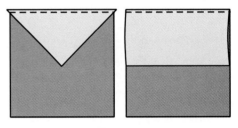

Fig 11

Place flap backing right sides together with flap; sew along remaining unsewn sides (two short sides for a triangle and two short and one long side for rectangle), **Fig 12**. Turn flap right side out. Press raw edge of flap back under ¼" and topstitch or whipstitch closed, **Fig 13**.

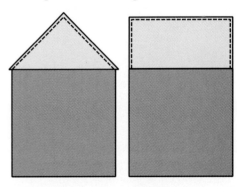

Fig 12

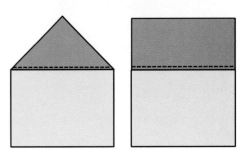

Fig 13

Sew a zigzag stitch across top edge of pillow front. *Note: Pillow front can be patchwork or a cut piece of fabric.* Fold zigzagged edge ¼" toward wrong side; stitch near fold, **Fig 14**.

Fig 14

Place pillow front right sides together with pillow back. Sew along remaining three sides making sure that flap is out flat so it doesn't get caught in your stitching, **Fig 15**. Sew a zigzag stitch along edge of seams for a nice finish.

Fig 15

Turn pillow right side out. Place pillow form through opening. Fold flap over. Attach end of flap to pillow front with buttons, bows, snaps, or hook and loop fastener such as Velcro. With this flap, you will be able to remove the pillow form for easy cleaning of pillow.

Optional: *For a permanently closed flap pillow, place flap front and flap backing right sides together. Sew along both short sides. Trim seam allowance at corner(s) and turn flap right side out. Place flap along top edge of pillow front, right side up, on right side of pillow front; pin in place. Position pillow backing right sides together with top/flap; sew along all four sides leaving 10" opening at bottom edge.* **Note:** *Be sure flap is folded away from edges so it doesn't get caught in stitching. Turn pillow top right side out, push pillow form through opening and whipstitch opening closed. Add buttons for decorative purposes if desired.*

Pillows With Ruffles

Note: *Sizes of ruffles are given with individual pattern instructions.*

Some of the pillows have ruffles. You can use purchased ruffles or you can make one from coordinating fabric. To make a ruffle, sew ruffle strips end to end diagonally to make one long strip, **Fig 16**. Cut excess ¼" from seam, **Fig 17**.

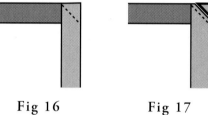

Fig 16   Fig 17

Sew ends together in same manner to form a ring, **Fig 18**.

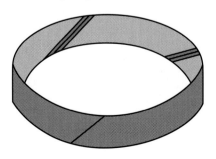

Fig 18

Fold ruffle in half lengthwise with wrong sides together, **Fig 19**; press.

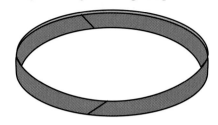

Fig 19

Divide the ruffle into four equal sections; use a pin to mark each section, **Fig 20**.

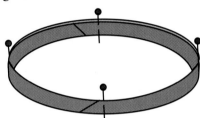

Fig 20

Beginning and ending at each pin, sew two rows of long basting stitches ¼" and ⅛" from raw edge of ruffle, **Fig 21**.

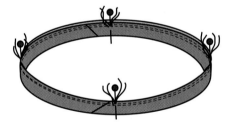

Fig 21

Mark the midpoint of each side of pillow top, **Fig 22**.

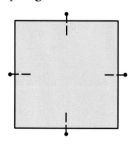

Fig 22

Place ruffle on right side of pillow top, matching pins on ruffle with pins on pillow top, **Fig 23**.

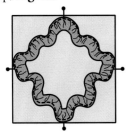

Fig 23

Pull stitches to gather ruffle between pins, **Fig 24**. Pin in place. ***Note:*** *Be sure to make ruffle gathers as even as possible and curved at each corner.*

Fig 24

Baste ruffle to pillow top using ¼" seam allowance.

Place pillow top and backing right sides together (ruffle will be in between); pin in place. Sew along all four sides, leaving a 10"–12" opening for turning, **Fig 25**. ***Note:*** *Be sure not to catch ruffle in stitching.*

Fig 25

Turn pillow right side out through opening. Place pillow form through opening and whipstitch opening closed.

Pillows With Back Opening

You may want to make a pillow that you can remove easily for cleaning. By making a two-piece backing, you can replace the pillow form easily without removing any sewing.

Cut pillow backing fabric into two equal pieces. To figure out the size to cut your backing, divide the backing size given in the individual instructions in half, then add 5". For example, if the instructions say to cut backing 14½" square, divide that number by 2 and you will get 7¼". Add 5" to that measurement for a cut size of 12¼" x 14½".

Fold one 14½" edge ¼" toward wrong side; fold another ½" and press.

Sew along first fold, **Fig 26**.

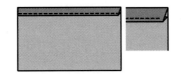

Fig 26

Repeat for other backing piece. ***Note:*** *If you would like a secure closure, see options below.*

Overlap backing pieces right sides up so that both pieces together equal the measurement of the pillow backing given in the individual pattern instructions (in the example above, 14½" x 14½"), **Fig 27**.

Fig 27

Baste sides together and treat as one piece.

Place backing and pillow front right sides together. Sew along all four sides. Turn pillow right side out through opening in backing.

Optional Closures

The opening will lay flat and stay closed, but if you would like a more secure closure, use one of the following options prior to basting the backing pieces together:

• *Sew hook and loop fasteners such as Velcro to open edges of backing for a secure closure.*

• *Sew three or four buttons to hemmed edge of one piece and buttonholes to match on remaining piece.*

• *Sew three or four large snaps to hemmed edge of both pieces.*

Modern Geometric

This group of pillows, with its more geometric look, will fit in with a modern decor.

Tassel

Pillow Size: 14" square
Technique: Stitch & Flip, page 6

Materials

½ yd lt print (includes backing)
Fat quarter, paisley border print
4"-long beaded tassel
2 yds cording
14" pillow form

Cutting

1 – 6½" x 14½" strip, paisley border print
2 – 4½" x 14½" strips, lt print
2 – 3½" squares, lt print
1 – 14½" square, lt print (backing)

Instructions

1. Using the stitch and flip method, sew two lt print squares to one end of 6½" x 14½" paisley border print strip, **Fig 1**.

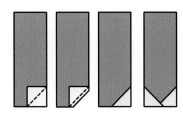

Fig 1

2. Sew 4½" x 14½" lt print strips to each side of border print strip, **Fig 2**.

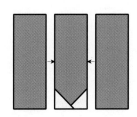

Fig 2

3. Refer to Pillows With Trimmed Edges, page 12, to finish pillow.

4. Referring to photograph, attach tassel at point of center panel.

Fancy Star

Pillow Size: 14" square
Technique: Stitch & Flip, page 6

Materials

Fat quarters, rust, rust/green print, dk green, lt green
½ yd ecru (includes backing)
14" pillow form
2 yds trim

Cutting

1 – 4" square, rust (A)
2 – 4½" squares cut in half diagonally, rust, (B)
4 – 2¼" x 4" rectangles, rust (C)
8 – 2¼" squares, rust/green print (D)
2 – 3⅞" squares cut in half diagonally, dk green (E)
4 – 4" squares, dk green (F)
4 – 2¼" squares, lt green (G)
8 – 2¼" x 4" rectangles, ecru (H)
4 – 3⅛" squares cut in half diagonally, ecru (I)
16 – 2¼" squares, ecru (J)
1 – 14½" square, ecru (backing)

Instructions

1. Sew I triangle to adjacent sides of a G square, **Fig 3**.

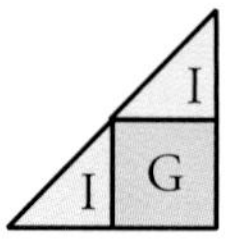

Fig 3

2. Sew B triangle to diagonal edge, **Fig 4**.

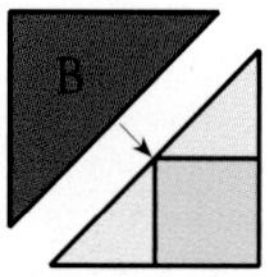

Fig 4

3. Place H rectangles right sides together; cut corner at a 45-degree angle, **Fig 5**.

Fig 5

4. Sew H to adjacent sides of unit from step 2, **Fig 6**.

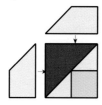

Fig 6

5. Sew E triangle to diagonal edge, **Fig 7**.

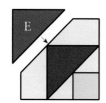

Fig 7

6. Repeat steps 1-5 three more times.

7. Using stitch and flip method, sew D squares to adjacent sides of F square, **Fig 8**.

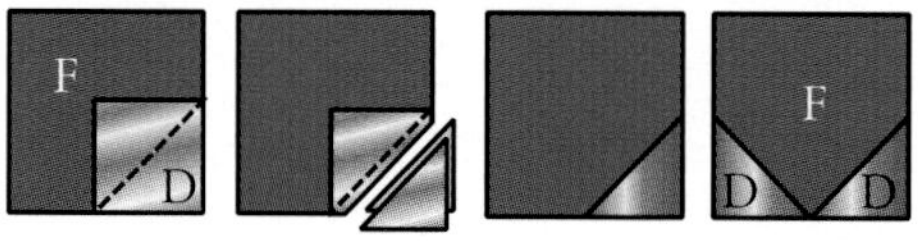

Fig 8

8. Using stitch and flip method, sew J squares to remaining sides of F square, **Fig 9**.

Fig 9

9. Using stitch and flip method, sew J squares to C rectangle, **Fig 10**.

Fig 10

10. Sew units from steps 8 and 9 together, **Fig 11**.

Fig 11

11. Repeat steps 7-10 three more times.

12. Place units and A square according to **Fig 12**. Sew together in rows; press seams for rows in alternating directions. Sew rows together to complete pillow top.

Fig 12

13. Refer to Basic Pillow, page 12, to finish pillow.

Framed Paisleys

Pillow Size: 12" square plus 2" flange
Technique: Stitch & Flip, page 6

Materials

Fat quarters, theme print, ecru, rust, gold, gold/ecru print
Fat quarter, backing fabric
12" pillow form

Cutting

1 – 8½" square, theme print (A)
4 – 4½" squares, rust (B)
4 – 2½" x 4½" rectangles, rust (C)
4 – 2⅞" squares, gold (D)
4 – 2½" squares, gold/ecru print (E)
8 – 2½" squares, ecru (F)
4 – 2⅞" squares, ecru (G)
2 – 2½" x 12½" strips, theme print
2 – 2½" x 16½" strips, theme print
1 – 16½" square, backing fabric

Instructions

1. Using stitch and flip method, sew B squares to all four corners of A square, **Fig 13**.

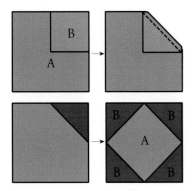

Fig 13

2. Using stitch and flip method, sew F squares to C rectangle, **Fig 14**. Repeat three more times.

Fig 14

3. Draw a diagonal line on wrong side of G squares. Place D and G squares right sides together. Sew ¼" from each side of diagonal line, **Fig 15**.

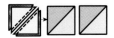

Fig 15

4. Cut along drawn line for two triangle/squares, **Fig 16**.

Fig 16

5. Sew triangle/square to each side of unit from step 2, **Fig 17**. Repeat three more times.

Fig 17

6. Sew unit from step 5 to opposite sides of A/B square, noting placement, **Fig 18**.

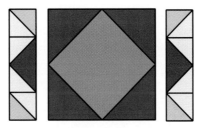

Fig 18

7. Sew E square to each end of remaining two units from step 5, then sew to opposite ends of pillow top, **Fig 19**.

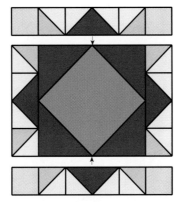

Fig 19

8. Sew 2½" x 12½" theme print strips to opposite sides of pillow top; sew 2½" x 16½" theme print strips to top and bottom to complete pillow top, **Fig 20**.

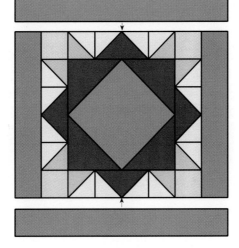

Fig 20

9. Refer to Pillows With a Flange, page 13, to finish pillow.

Woven Strips

Pillow Size: 16" square
Technique: Half-Square Triangles, page 5

Materials
Fat quarters, ecru, rust, green
Fat quarter, backing fabric
2 yds loop fringe
16" pillow form

Cutting
8 – 2½" squares, ecru
16 – 3" squares, ecru
8 – 2½" squares, green
12 – 3" squares, green
8 – 2½" squares, rust
12 – 3" squares, rust
1 – 16½" square, backing fabric

Instructions

1. Draw a diagonal line on wrong side of all 3" ecru squares.

2. Place 3" green and ecru squares right sides together; sew ¼" from each side of drawn line, **Fig 21**.

Fig 21

3. Cut along drawn line for two triangle/squares, **Fig 22**. Repeat with seven more pairs of squares for 16 green/ecru triangle/squares.

Fig 22

4. Place 3" rust and ecru squares right sides together; sew ¼" from each side of drawn line, **Fig 23**.

Fig 23

5. Cut along drawn line for two triangle/squares, **Fig 24**. Repeat with seven more pairs of squares for 16 rust/ecru triangle/squares.

Fig 24

6. Draw diagonal line on wrong side of remaining rust or green (whichever are lighter) squares. Place 3" rust and green squares right sides together; sew ¼" from each side of drawn line, **Fig 25**.

Fig 25

7. Cut along drawn line for two riangle/squares, **Fig 26**. Repeat with three more pairs of squares for 16 green/rust triangle/squares.

Fig 26

8. Trim all triangle/square to 2½".

9. Place squares and triangle/squares according to **Fig 27**.

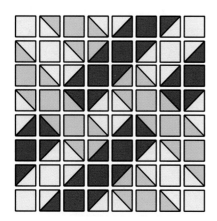

Fig 27

10. Sew together in pairs, then sew pairs together, **Fig 28**. Continue sewing in pairs until pillow top is complete.

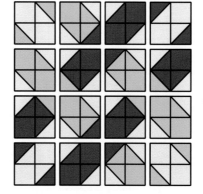

Fig 28

11. Refer to Pillows With Trimmed Edges, page 12, to complete pillow.

Round Cabin

Pillow Size: 14" round
Technique: Foundation Piecing, page 8

Materials
⅛ yd each green/rust (A), lt rust (B), med rust (C), dk rust (D), lt green (E), med green (F), dk green (G), background (H)
Fat quarter, backing fabric
14" round pillow form
2 yds cording

Cutting
Note: Foundation Piecing does not require cutting exact pieces, but you may cut 2¼"-wide strips of each fabric for easier piecing.

1 – 14½" Circle (page 21), backing fabric

Instructions

1. Refer to Foundation Piecing to make four sections using pattern on page 21. Note that each section has different color placement, **Fig 29**.

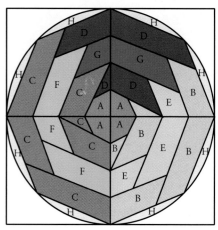

Fig 29

2. Sew sections together in pairs, then sew pairs together, **Fig 30**. Trim fabric ¼" from outside curved edge. Remove paper foundations.

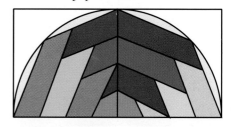

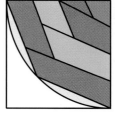 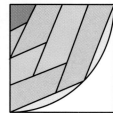

Fig 30

3. Refer to Pillows With Trimmed Edges, page 12, to finish pillow.

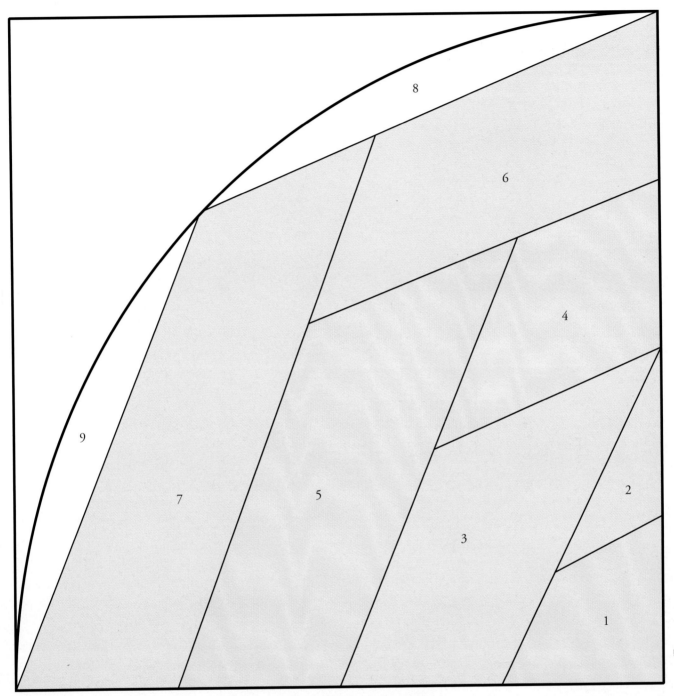

Round Cabin Foundation Pattern

Star Power

This group of pillows is sure to make your teenager feel like a star. There are two patchwork star blocks, as well as two foundation-pieced blocks. The neck-roll pillow has appliquéd stars on a dark celestial background.

Floating Star

Pillow Size: 14" square
Technique: Half-Square Triangles, page 5

Materials
Fat quarter, lt blue
10" square each dk blue, lt yellow, dk yellow, orange
Fat quarter, backing
14" pillow form
2 yds fringe trim

Cutting
4 – 4" squares, lt blue
4 – 4½" squares, lt blue
2 – 4½" squares, dk blue
3 – 4½" squares, dk yellow
1 – 4½" square, orange
2 – 4½" squares, lt yellow
1 – 14½" square, backing

Instructions

1. Draw a diagonal line on wrong side of each 4½" lt blue and lt yellow square, **Fig 1**.

Fig 1

2. Place a lt blue square right sides together with a dk blue square; sew ¼" from each side of drawn line, **Fig 2**. Cut along drawn line to get two triangle/squares, **Fig 3**. Repeat.

Fig 2

Fig 3

3. Place lt blue and dk yellow squares right sides together. Sew ¼" from drawn line. Cut along drawn line for two triangle/squares, **Fig 4**. Repeat.

Fig 4

4. Place dk yellow and lt yellow squares right sides together. Sew ¼" from drawn line. Cut along drawn line for two triangle/squares, **Fig 5**.

Fig 5

5. Place lt yellow and orange squares right sides together. Sew ¼" from drawn line. Cut along drawn line for two triangle/squares, **Fig 6**.

Fig 6

6. Arrange squares and triangle/squares according to **Fig 7**. Sew together in rows; press seams in opposite directions for adjacent rows. Sew rows together to complete pillow top.

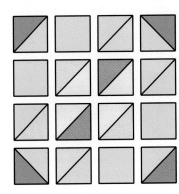

Fig 7

7. See Pillows With Trimmed Edges, page 12, to complete pillow.

Pinwheel Star

Pillow Size: 14" square
Technique: Half-Square Triangles, page 5

Materials

Fat quarter, lt blue
10" square each dk blue, dk yellow, lt yellow, orange
Fat quarter, backing
14" pillow form
2 yds corded fringe trim

Cutting

2 – 4½" squares, dk blue
6 – 4½" squares, lt blue
4 – 4½" squares, dk yellow
2 – 4½" squares, lt yellow
2 – 4½" squares, orange
1 – 14½" square, backing

Instructions

1. Draw a diagonal line on wrong side of all lt blue and lt yellow squares, **Fig 8**.

Fig 8

2. Place lt blue square right sides together with dk blue square; sew ¼" from each side of drawn line, **Fig 9**. Cut along drawn

Fig 9

---

line to get two triangle/squares, **Fig 10**. Repeat.

Fig 10

3. Place dk yellow square right sides together with lt blue square; sew ¼" from each side of drawn line. Cut along drawn line to get two triangle/squares, **Fig 11**. Repeat three more times.

Fig 11

4. Place lt yellow and orange squares right sides together; sew ¼" from each side of drawn line. Cut along drawn line to get two triangle/squares, **Fig 12**. Repeat.

Fig 12

5. Arrange triangle/squares according to **Fig 13**. Sew together in rows; press seams in opposite directions for adjacent rows. Sew rows together to complete pillow top.

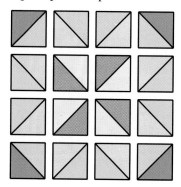

Fig 13

6. Refer to Pillows With Trimmed Edges, page 12, to finish pillow.

Crazy Star

Pillow Size: 12" with 2" flange

Materials

Fat quarter, yellow
Scraps, assorted blue fabrics
½ yd dk blue (flange and backing)
12" pillow form

Cutting

Note: Foundation piecing does not require cutting exact pieces.

2 – 1½" x 10½" strips, yellow (border)
2 – 1½" x 12½" strips, yellow (border)
2 – 2½" x 12½" strips, dk blue (flange)
2 – 2½" x 16½" strips, dk blue (flange)
1 – 16½" square, backing fabric

Instructions

1. Refer to Foundation Piecing and use pattern on pages 28 and 29 to make Crazy Star block, **Fig 14**.

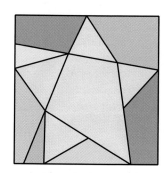

Fig 14

2. Sew 1½" x 10½" yellow strips to sides of block; press seams toward border. Sew 1½" x 12½" yellow strips to top and bottom, **Fig 15**; press seams toward border.

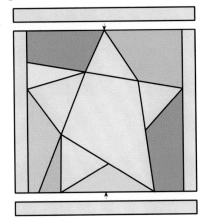

Fig 15

3. Sew 2½" x 12½" dk blue strips to sides and 2½" x 16½" dk blue strips to top and bottom of block, **Fig 16**. Press seams toward border.

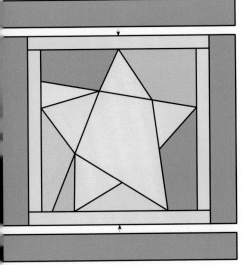

Fig 16

4. Refer to Pillows With a Flange, page 13, to complete pillow.

Comforting Stars

Pillow Size: 14" x 5" neck roll
Technique Used: Easy Machine Appliqué, page 7

Materials

1 yd dk blue
¼ yd yellow
5" x 14" neck-roll pillow form
1½ yds cording, ribbon or fabric strips

Cutting

Note: Refer to Easy Machine Appliqué to cut out assorted stars, page 26, from yellow fabric.

1 Large Star, yellow
2 Medium Stars, yellow
3 Medium-small Star, yellow
2 Small Stars, yellow
1 – 14½" x 19½" rectangle, dk blue
2 – 6½" x 19½" rectangles, dk blue

Instructions

1. Place stars in a pleasing arrangement on 14½" x 19½" dk blue rectangle, **Fig 17**. Fuse in place referring to manufacturer's directions. Machine-zigzag around stars if desired.

Fig 17

2. Sew 6½" x 19½" dk blue strip to each side of star panel, **Fig 18**. Press seams toward strips.

Fig. 18

3. Fold pillow top in half crosswise with right sides together to form a tube. Sew along edge across from fold using ¼" seam allowance, **Fig 19**.

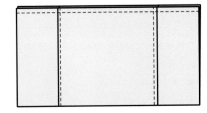

Fig 19

4. For sides, fold raw edges under ¼", then fold again, **Fig 20**. Stitch near first fold, **Fig 21**.

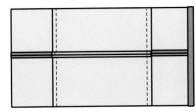

Fig 20

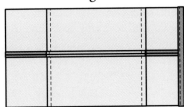

Fig 21

5. Turn pillow top right side out. Place pillow form centered inside. Tie open edges with cording, ribbon or even fabric strips to finish pillow.

Stargazing Floor Pillow

Pillow Size: 30" square
Technique: Foundation Piecing, page 8

Materials

¼ yd each yellow, orange
⅜ yd lt blue
1⅜ yds dk blue (includes backing)
30" pillow form

Cutting

Note: *Foundation piecing does not require exact cutting of fabric shapes.*

2 – 4½" x 28½" strips, dk blue (border)
2 – 4½" x 36½" strips, dk blue (border)
1 – 36½" square, dk blue (backing)

Instructions

1. Make 16 blocks using pattern on page 27 and referring to Foundation Piecing, **Fig 22**.

Fig 22

2. Place blocks according to **Fig 23**. Sew together in rows; press seams for rows in opposite directions. Sew rows together.

Fig 23

3. Sew 4½" x 28½" dk blue strips to sides of pillow top; press seams toward strips. Sew 4½" x 36½" strips to top and bottom, **Fig 24**; press seams toward strips.

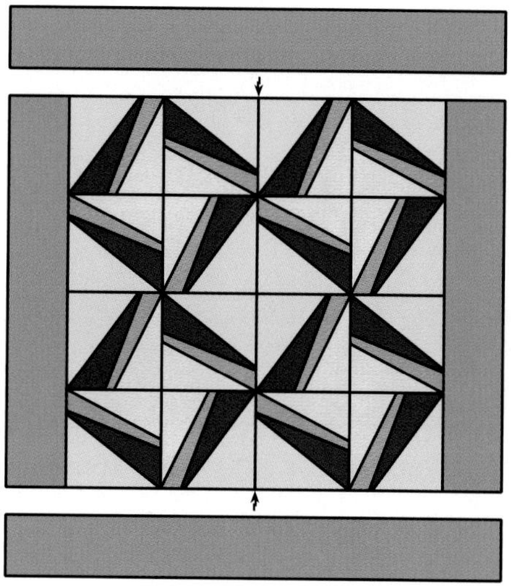

Fig 24

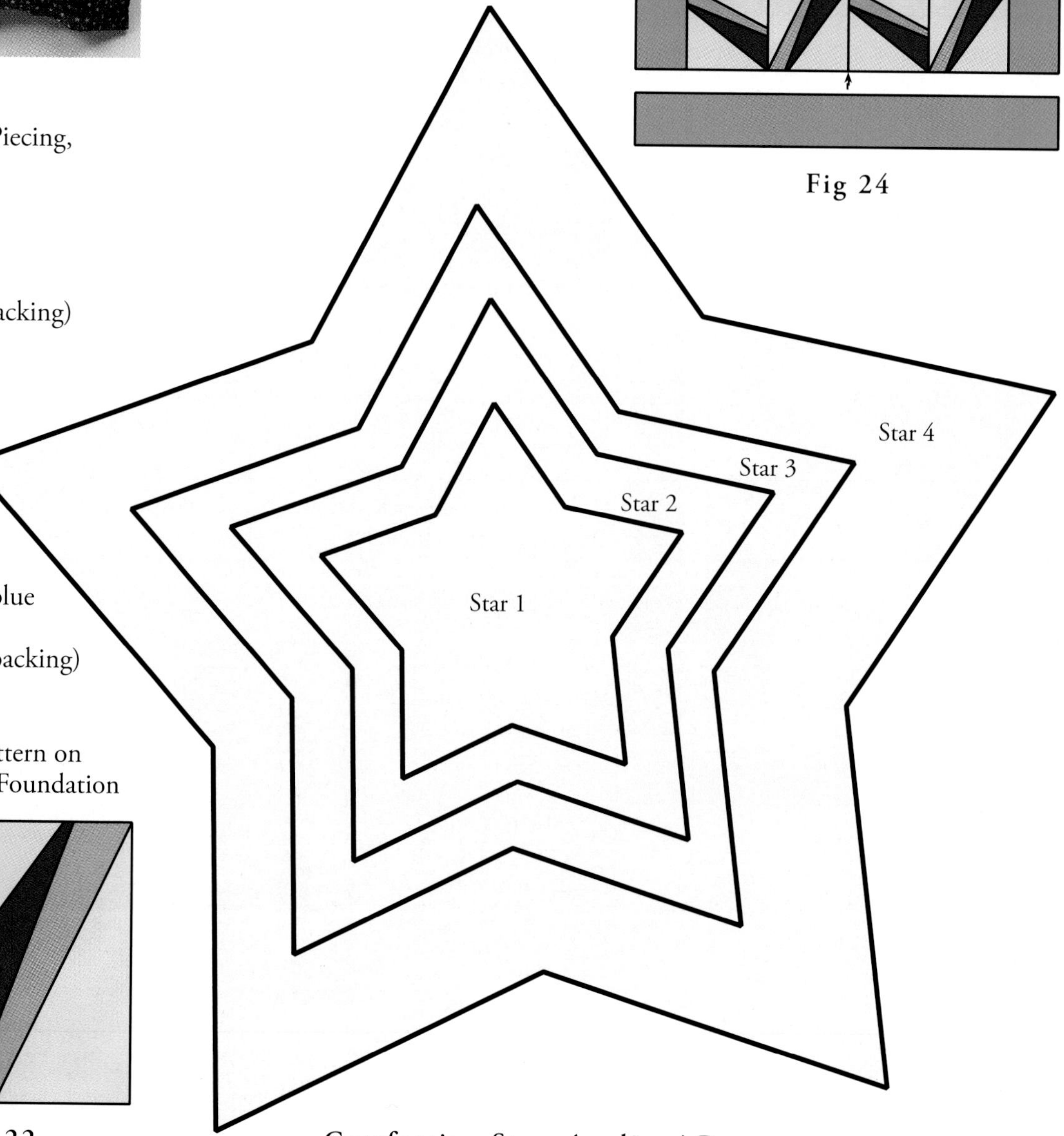

Star 1
Star 2
Star 3
Star 4

Comforting Stars Appliqué Patterns

4. Refer to Pillows With a Flange, page 13, to complete pillow. ***Note:*** *When making flange, sew 3" from outside edge of pillow top rather than in actual seam,* ***Fig 25.***

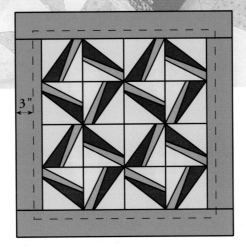

Fig 25

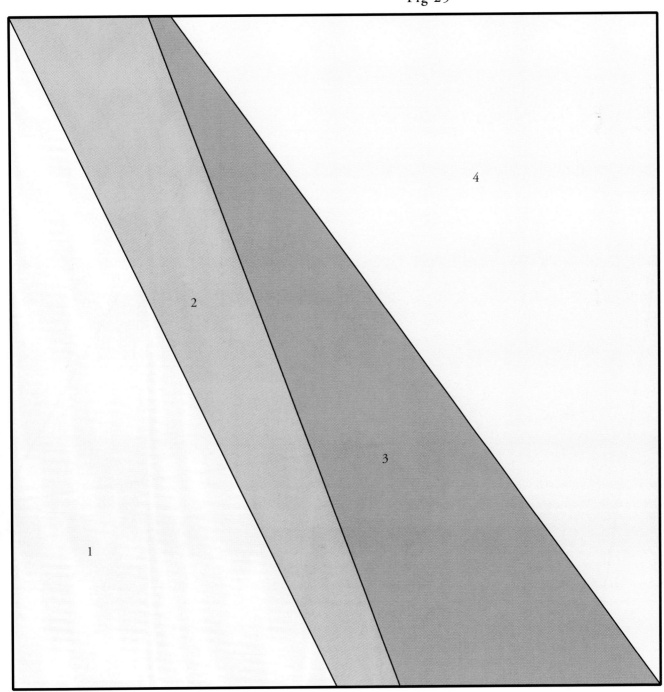

Stargazing Foundation Pattern

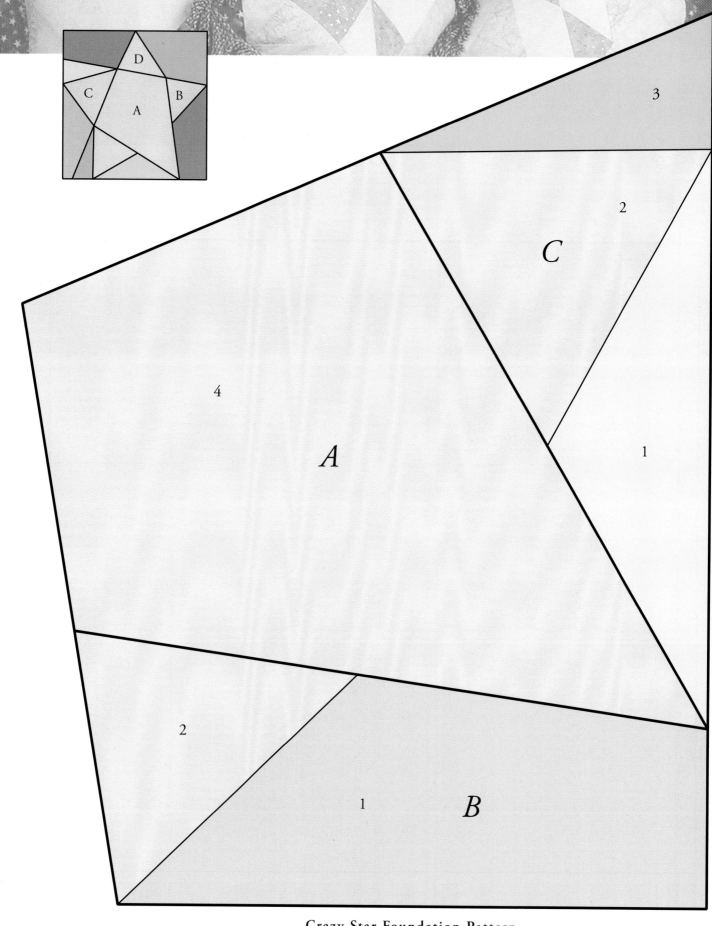

Crazy Star Foundation Pattern

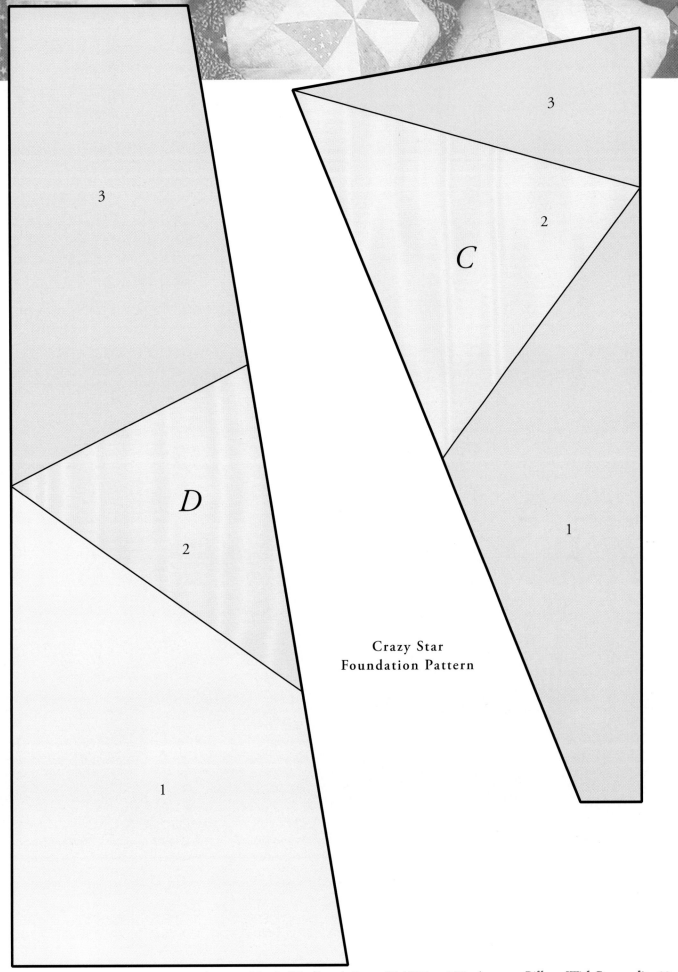

D

3

2

1

C

3

2

1

Crazy Star
Foundation Pattern

Tulip Treasures

Brighten a living room or bedroom with this colorful collection of pillows with a tulip theme.
There are four pillows to choose from, so make one or make them all!

Tulip Garden

Pillow Size: 12" x 16" rectangle
Technique: Stitch & Flip, page 6

Materials

Fat quarters, lt blue, pink, dk green,
   med green, lt green, lt blue
Fat quarter, backing fabric
12" x 16" pillow form
2 yds trim

Cutting

4 – 2½" x 4½" rectangles, lt blue
8 – 2" squares, lt blue
2 – 4½" squares, lt blue
4 – 2½" x 4½" rectangles, pink
8 – 2½" squares, pink
6 – 1½" x 4½" rectangles, dk green
6 – 2" x 4½" rectangles, med green
4 – 2" squares, med green
4 – 2" squares, lt green
6 – 2" x 4½" rectangles, lt green
1 – 12½" x 16½" rectangle, backing
   fabric

Instructions

1. Sew med green, dk green and lt green rectangles together for stem squares, **Fig 1**. Repeat five more times. Press seams toward dk green for four of the squares and toward the lt and med green on the remaining two.

Fig 1

2. Draw diagonal line on wrong side of 2" lt blue squares. Using the stitch and flip technique, place lt blue square right side down on stem square with seams pressed toward dk green; sew along drawn line, **Fig 2**.

Fig 2

3. Trim ¼" from seam and flip triangle over, **Fig 3**.

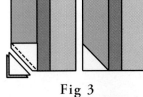

Fig 3

4. Repeat on opposite corner, **Fig 4**.

5. Repeat steps 2-4 for three more stem squares.

Fig 4

6. Draw diagonal line on wrong side of 2½" pink squares. Sew two 2½" pink squares to each 2½" x 4½" lt blue rectangle using the stitch and flip method, **Fig 5**.

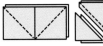

Fig 5

7. Draw diagonal line on wrong side of 2" med green and lt green squares. Sew one of each color onto each 2½" x 4½" pink rectangle, **Fig 6**.

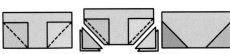

Fig 6

8. Sew units from steps 6 and 7 together to form tulip, **Fig 7**.

9. Place tulip squares, stem squares and lt blue squares according to **Fig 8**. Sew together in rows, then sew rows together.

Fig 7

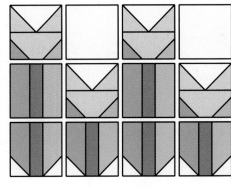

Fig 8

10. Refer to Pillows With Trimmed Edges, page 12, to finish pillow.

Tulip Nine-Patch

Pillow Size: 12" square plus flange
Technique: Stitch & Flip, page 6

Materials
Fat quarters, yellow, pink, purple, green, lt blue
½ yd floral print (includes flange and backing)
12" pillow form

Cutting
4 – 4½" squares, floral print
2 – 2½" x 4½" rectangles each, pink and yellow
1 – 2½" x 4½" rectangle, purple
4 – 2½" squares each, pink and yellow
2 – 2½" squares, purple
5 – 2½" x 4½" rectangles, lt blue
10 – 2" squares, green
2 – 2½" x 12½" strips, floral print
2 – 2½" x 16½" strips, floral print

Instructions

1. Using the stitch and flip technique, sew 2½" pink, purple or yellow squares to lt blue rectangles, **Fig 9**; cut ¼" from drawn line and flip triangles over, **Fig 10**.

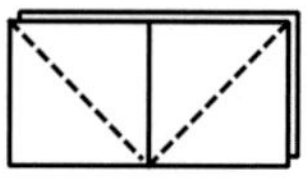

Fig 9

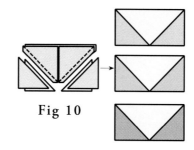

Fig 10

2. Repeat step 1 with 2" green squares and pink, purple and yellow rectangles, **Fig 11**.

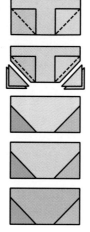

Fig 11

3. Sew rectangles from step 1 and step 2 together, matching colors, to form tulips, **Fig 12**.

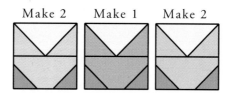

Make 2   Make 1   Make 2

Fig 12

4. Arrange floral print squares and tulips according to **Fig 13**. Sew together in rows; press seams for rows in alternating directions. Sew rows together to form Nine Patch.

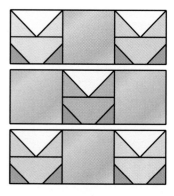

Fig 13

5. Sew 2½" x 12½" strips to sides of Nine-Patch; press seams toward strips. Sew 2½" x 16½" strips to top and bottom of Nine-Patch, **Fig 14**; press seams toward strips.

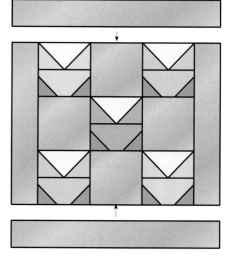

Fig 14

6. Refer to Pillows With a Flange, page 13, to finish pillow.

Tulip Flap Pillow

Pillow Size: 12" square
Technique: Foundation Piecing, page 8

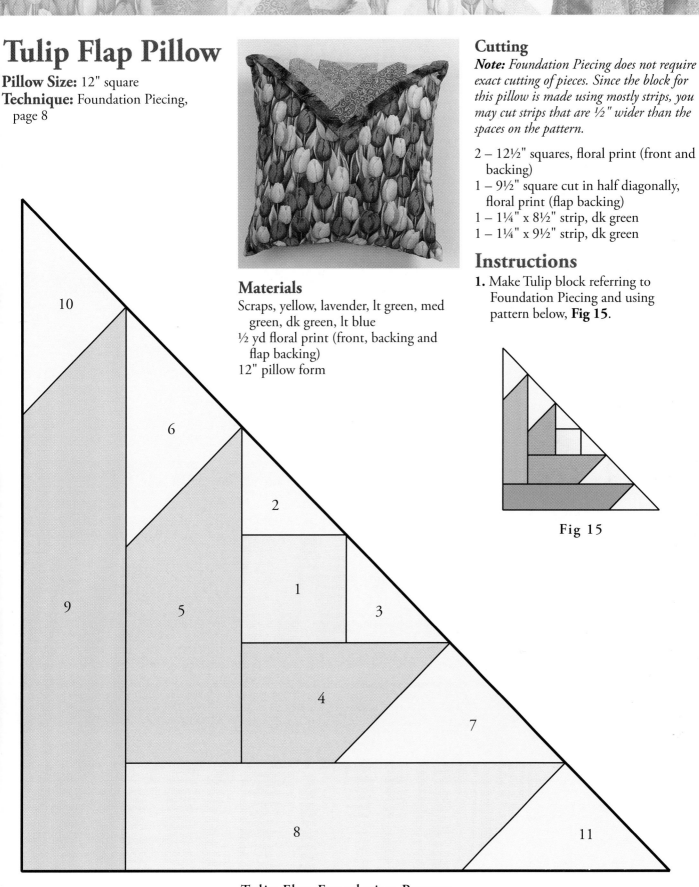

Materials
Scraps, yellow, lavender, lt green, med green, dk green, lt blue
½ yd floral print (front, backing and flap backing)
12" pillow form

Cutting
Note: *Foundation Piecing does not require exact cutting of pieces. Since the block for this pillow is made using mostly strips, you may cut strips that are ½" wider than the spaces on the pattern.*

2 – 12½" squares, floral print (front and backing)
1 – 9½" square cut in half diagonally, floral print (flap backing)
1 – 1¼" x 8½" strip, dk green
1 – 1¼" x 9½" strip, dk green

Instructions
1. Make Tulip block referring to Foundation Piecing and using pattern below, **Fig 15**.

Fig 15

Tulip Flap Foundation Pattern

2. Sew 1¼" x 8½" dk green strip to short side of Tulip block; press seam toward strip. Sew 1¼" x 9½" strip to adjacent short side, **Fig 16**; press seam toward strip. Trim ends even with diagonal edge, **Fig 17**.

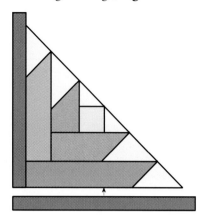

Fig 16

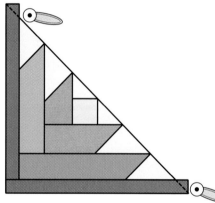

Fig 17

3. Remove paper foundation.

4. Refer to Pillows With a Flap, page 13, to finish pillow.

Tulips in the Round

Pillow Size: 14" round
Technique: Foundation Piecing, page 8

Materials

Fat quarters, lt pink, dk pink
½ yd green (includes backing)
14" round pillow form
2 yds ruffle or three 3½"-wide strips, pink

Cutting

Note: Foundation piecing does not require cutting of exact pieces, but you may cut the following strips for easier piecing:

2 – 3"-wide strips each, lt pink and dk pink
1 – 2½"-wide strip, green
1 – 3¼"-wide strip, green
Optional square pillow:
2 – 2¼"-wide strips, green

Instructions

1. Make four Tulips referring to Foundation Piecing and using pattern on page 35, **Fig 18**.

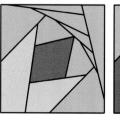

Fig 18

Note: This pattern allows you to make a 14" square in addition to the 14" round pillow. To make the round pillow you will need to trim block ¼" from red line. The red curved line on the pattern will be used as the sewing line.

2. Sew the tulip blocks together in pairs, then sew pairs together, **Fig 19**.

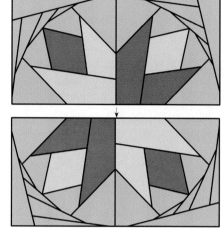

Fig 19

3. Trim ¼" from red curved line, **Fig 20**.

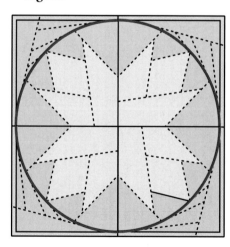

Fig 20

4. Refer to Pillows With Trimmed Edges, page 12, to finish pillow. *Note: Sew along red curved line of foundation when sewing the pillow top and backing together; remove paper foundations, then turn right side out and finish pillow.*

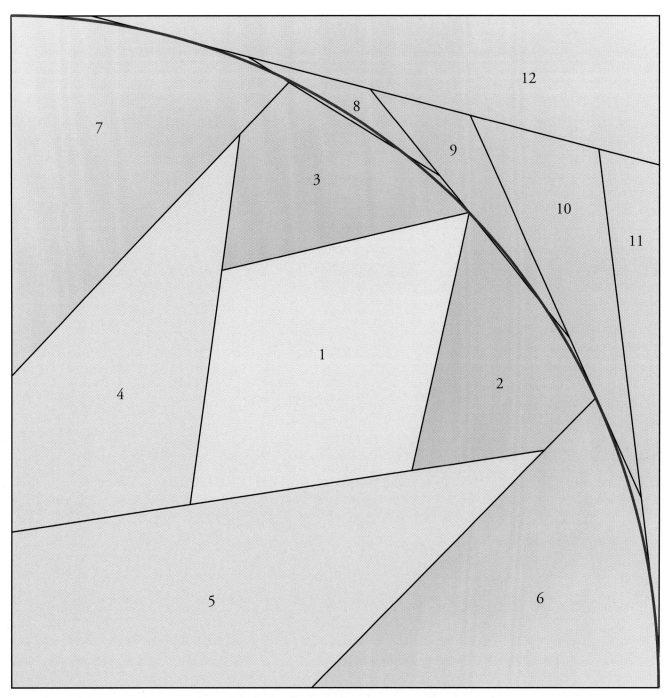

Tulips in the Round Foundation Pattern

Tropical Paradise

Surround yourself with brightly colored pillows depicting palm trees,
pineapples, flowers and ocean waves as you dream of a tropical paradise!

Palm Tree Island

Pillow Size: 14" square
Technique: Easy Machine Appliqué,
  page 7

Materials
½ yd background print (includes
  backing)
Scraps, brown, blue, green, beige, lt
  orange
14" pillow form
½ yd paper-backed fusible web
2 yds beaded trim

Cutting
Note: *See Easy Machine Appliqué to cut*
  out patterns found on page 38.
1 – Sun, lt orange
1 – Island, beige
1 – Trunk, brown
1 – Palm Leaves, green
1 – 5½" x 14½" rectangle, blue (water)
2 – 14½" squares, background print

Instructions
1. Cut a slightly curved line along
one long edge of 5½" x 14½" blue
rectangle for Water. Fuse Water,
Island, Palm Leaves, Trunk and Sun
to background fabric referring to
Fig 1. Machine-zigzag around each
shape if desired.

Fig 1

2. Refer to Pillows With Trimmed
Edges, page 12, to finish pillow.

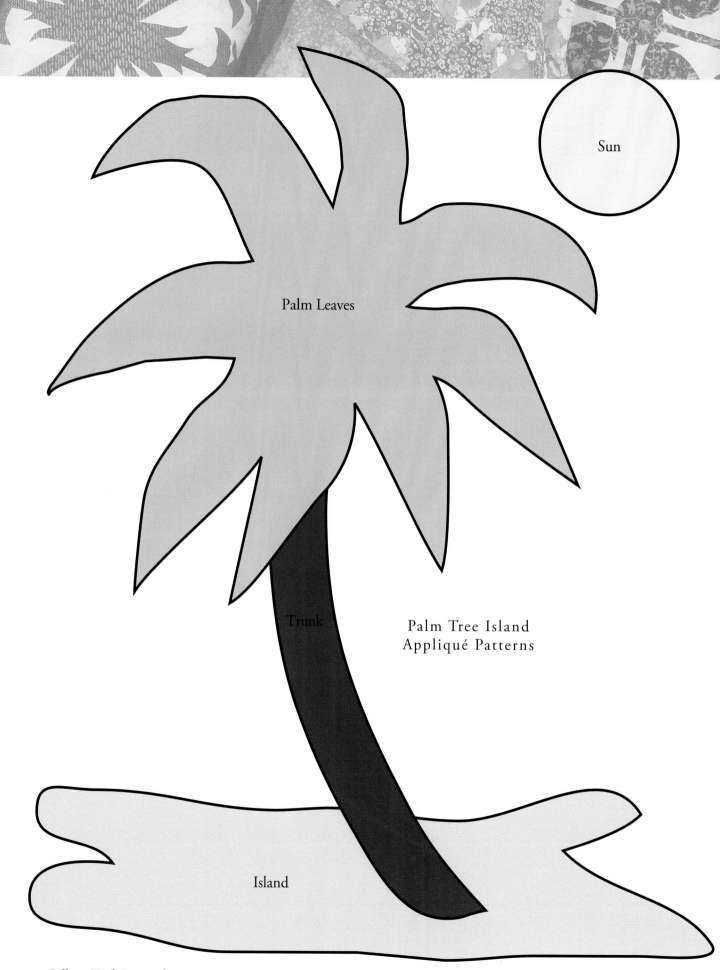

Sun

Palm Leaves

Trunk

Palm Tree Island
Appliqué Patterns

Island

Hawaiian Appliqué Pair

Pillow Size: 14" square
Technique: Easy Machine Appliqué, page 7

Materials

Note: *Materials given are for one pillow.*

½ yd background (includes backing)
Fat quarter, contrasting print
14" pillow form
2 yds cording
½ yd paper-backed fusible web

Cutting

Note: *See Easy Machine Appliqué, to cut out pattern found on page 40 or page 41.*

2 – 14½" squares, background print
1 – Pineapple or one Palm Tree design, contrasting print

Instructions

1. Trace block pattern in upper right corner of paper-backed fusible web, **Fig 2**.

Fig 2

2. Turn pattern a quarter turn, counter-clockwise and place next to pattern just drawn. Trace pattern again, **Fig 3**.

Fig 3

3. Trace pattern two more times, turning a quarter turn each time, to complete block, **Fig 4**.

Fig 4

4. Refer to Easy Machine Appliqué to cut and fuse shape to 14½" background fabric, **Fig 5**. Machine-zigzag around entire edge of appliqué if desired.

Fig 5

5. Refer to Pillows With Trimmed Edges, page 12, to finish pillow.

Hawaiian Pineapple Appliqué
Trace pattern four times,
rotating a quarter turn each time.

Hawaiian Palm Tree Appliqué
Trace pattern four times,
rotating a quarter turn each time.

Pineapple Pillow

Pillow Size: 14" with 2" flange
Technique: Foundation Piecing,
  page 8

Materials

Fat quarter, pink
¾ yd bright pink/orange print (includes
  flange and backing)
¼ yd blue/purple print
14" pillow form

Cutting

*Note: Although foundation piecing does
not require cutting exact pieces, you may
cut strips in the following widths to ease
construction.*

3⅛" strip, pink (space 1)
1¼"-wide strips, blue/purple print
  (spaces 6-9 and 14-17 and 22-25)
1½"-wide strips, blue/purple print
  (spaces 22-25)
1½"-wide strips, bright pink/orange
  print (spaces 2–5, 10-13 and 18-21)

1¾"-wide strips, bright pink/orange
  print (spaces 26-29)
2 – 2½" x 14½" strips, bright pink/
  orange print (flange)
2 – 2½" x 18½" strips, bright pink/
  orange print (flange)
1 – 18½" square, backing

Instructions

1. Refer to Foundation Piecing to make
   four blocks using pattern on page 43,
   Fig 6.

Fig 6

2. Sew blocks together in pairs, then
   sew pairs together, **Fig 7**. Remove
   paper foundations.

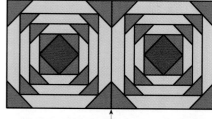

Fig 7

3. Sew 2½" x 14½" strips to sides;
   sew 2½" x 18½" strips to top and
   bottom, **Fig 8**.

4. Refer to Pillows With a Flange, page
   13, to finish pillow.

Fig 8

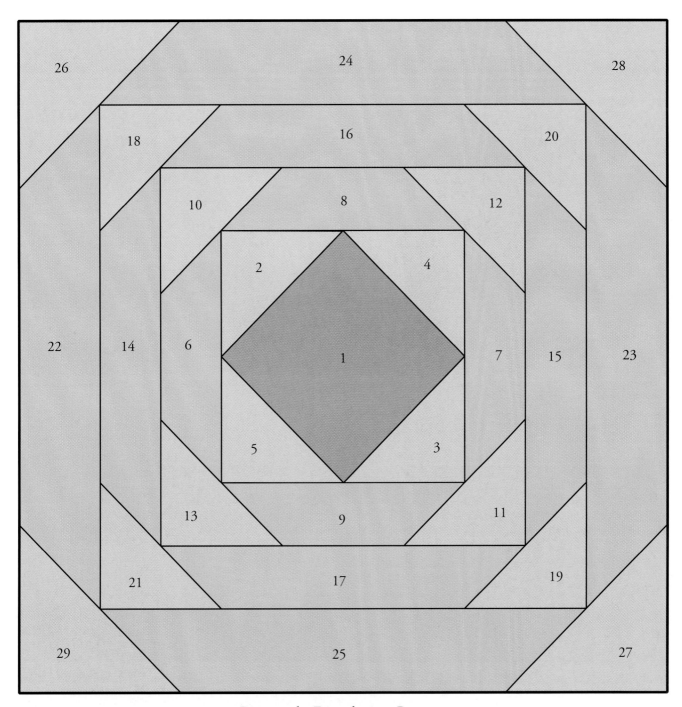

Pineapple Foundation Pattern

Bird of Paradise Block Pillow

Pillow Size: 14" square
Technique: Rotary Cutting, page 4

Materials

Fat quarters, lt orange, dk orange, green
½ yd backing
14" pillow form

Cutting

6 – 2½" squares, lt orange
6 – 2½" squares, dk orange
8 – 2½" squares, green
4 – 4½" squares, green
2 – 2¾" x 5⅜" rectangles, lt orange
2 – 2¾" x 5⅜" rectangles, dk orange
2 – 1½" x 12½" strips, border fabric
2 – 1½" x 14½" strips, border fabric
1 – 14½" square, backing

Instructions

1. Sew lt orange and green squares together, **Fig 9**; repeat. Sew pairs together to form a Four-Patch, **Fig 10**. Repeat for another Four-Patch.

Fig 9

Fig 10

2. Repeat step 1 with dk orange and green squares, **Fig 11**.

Fig 11

3. Sew lt orange and dk orange squares together; repeat. Sew pairs together to form Four-Patch, **Fig 12**.

Fig 12

4. On wrong side of 4½" green squares, draw a line from the top center to the lower left corner and a line from top center to lower right corner, **Fig 13**.

Fig 13

5. Cut ¼" from drawn lines, **Fig 14**.

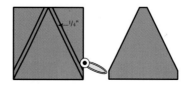

Fig 14

6. Place lt orange 2¾" x 5⅜" rectangles right sides together; cut diagonally to form triangles, **Fig 15**. *Note: There will be four triangles, two of which are mirror images of the other two.*

Fig 15

7. Repeat for dk orange rectangles, **Fig 16**.

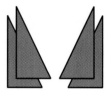

Fig 16

8. Sew lt orange triangle to left diagonal edge of green triangle; sew dk orange triangle to right diagonal edge, **Fig 17**. Repeat. Trim squares to 4½"

Fig 17

9. Repeat step 8, switching positions of lt and dk orange triangles, **Fig 18**.

Fig 18

10. Arrange squares and Four-Patches according to **Fig 19**. Sew together in rows; press seams for rows in alternating directions. Sew rows together.

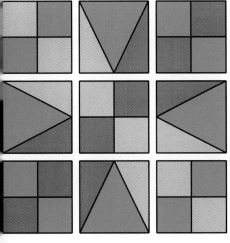

Fig 19

11. Sew 1½" x 12½" border strips to sides; sew 1½" x 14½" border strips to top and bottom, **Fig 20**.

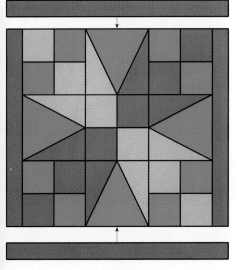

Fig 20

12. Refer to Basic Pillow, page 12, to finish pillow.

Ocean Waves

Pillow Size: 14" square
Technique: Half-Square Triangles, page 5

Materials

Fat quarters, turquoise and blue
Fat quarter, backing fabric
14" pillow form
2 yds purchased ruffle or three 3½"-wide strips, blue

Cutting

8 – 4½" squares, turquoise
8 – 4½" squares, blue
1 – 14½" square, backing

Instructions

1. Draw diagonal line on wrong side of turquoise squares, **Fig 21**.

Fig 21

2. Place turquoise and blue squares right sides together; sew ¼" from each side of drawn line, **Fig 22**.

Fig 22

3. Cut squares along drawn line to form two triangle/squares, **Fig 23**.

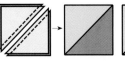

Fig 23

4. Repeat with remaining turquoise and blue squares.

5. Place triangle/squares according to **Fig 24**. Sew together in rows; press seams for rows in alternating directions. Sew rows together.

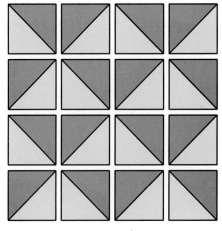

Fig 24

6. Refer to Pillows With Trimmed Edges, page 12, or Pillows With Ruffle, page 14, to finish pillow.

Perky Pansies

*Pansies, with their bright perky colors, are the perfect accent to any garden.
Why not bring them into your home to add a splash of color to your décor?*

Pretty Pansy

Pillow Size: 14" round
Technique: Easy Machine Appliqué,
page 7

Materials
Fat quarters, white, dk purple, reddish
  purple, med purple, lt purple
Scrap, yellow
½ yd floral print (includes backing)
14" round pillow form
½ yd paper-backed fusible web

Cutting
*Note: Refer to Easy Machine Appliqué to
cut out pieces with paper-backed fusible web
as noted on patterns on pages 48 and 49.*

2 – 14½" Circles, floral print
1 and 1 reversed – Lower Petal A,
  reddish purple
1 – Lower Petal B, white
1 – Lower Petal C, dk purple
2 and 2 reversed – Upper Petal A, lt purple
1 and 1 reversed – Upper Petal B,
  med purple
1 and 1 reversed – Upper Petal C, white
1 and 1 reversed – Upper Petal D, dk purple
1 – Center, yellow

Instructions

1. For right Upper
Petal B, remove
paper backing
from white Upper
Petal C and dk
purple Upper
Petal D; following
manufacturer's
directions, fuse to
med purple Upper
Petal B Petal, **Fig 3**.

Fig 3

2. Place fused Upper
Petal B right sides
together with
reversed Upper
Petal B; sew along
drawn line of entire
curved edge, **Fig 4**.
Turn right side out and press.

Fig 4

3. Place Upper Petal A right sides
together with reversed Upper Petal A;
sew along drawn line of entire curved
edge, **Fig 5**. Turn right side out. Place
Upper Petal B/C/D and Upper Petal
A together, **Fig 6**;
pin or baste in
place.

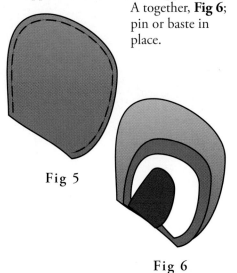

Fig 5

Fig 6

4. Repeat steps 1–3
for left Upper
Petal, **Fig 7**.

5. For Lower
Petal, remove
paper packing
from dk purple
Lower Petal
C and white
Lower Petal
B; following
manufacturer's directions, fuse to
reddish purple Lower Petal A, **Fig 8**.

Fig 7

Fig 8

6. Place fused Lower Petal A/B/C right
sides together with reversed Lower
Petal A; sew along drawn line of
  entire edge,
  Fig 9.

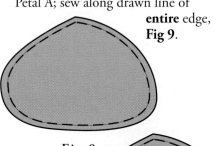

Fig 9

7. Separate
top and
bottom
layer and
cut a small
slit in **backing
only** of Lower
Petal A, **Fig 10**.

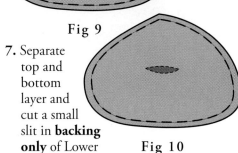

Fig 10

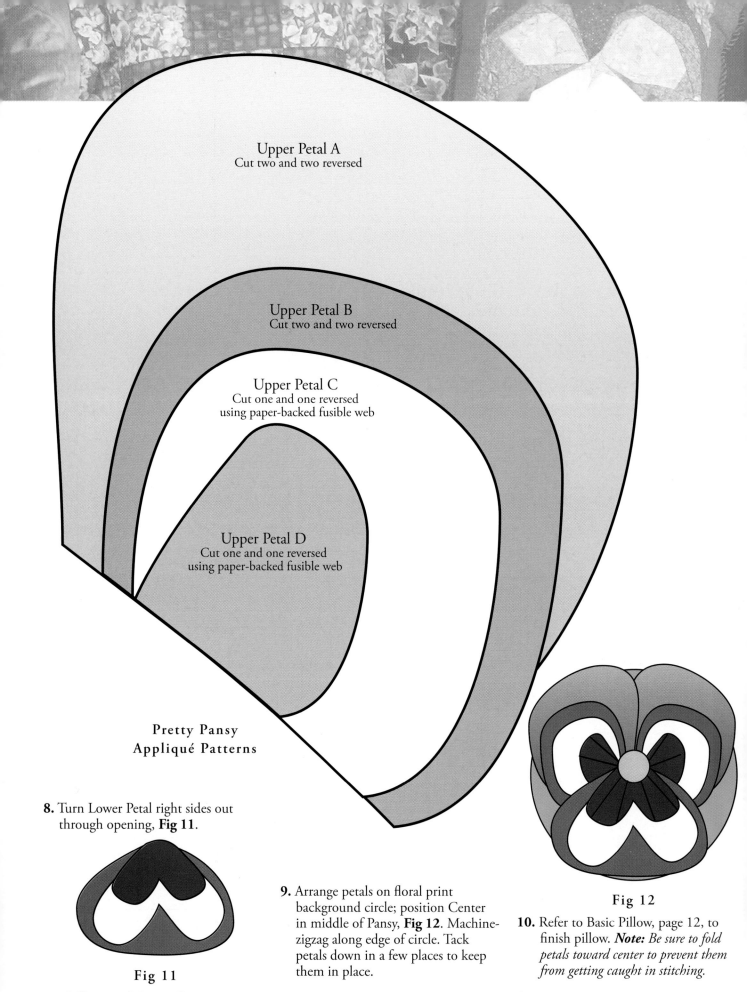

Upper Petal A
Cut two and two reversed

Upper Petal B
Cut two and two reversed

Upper Petal C
Cut one and one reversed
using paper-backed fusible web

Upper Petal D
Cut one and one reversed
using paper-backed fusible web

Pretty Pansy
Appliqué Patterns

8. Turn Lower Petal right sides out through opening, **Fig 11**.

Fig 11

9. Arrange petals on floral print background circle; position Center in middle of Pansy, **Fig 12**. Machine-zigzag along edge of circle. Tack petals down in a few places to keep them in place.

Fig 12

10. Refer to Basic Pillow, page 12, to finish pillow. ***Note:*** *Be sure to fold petals toward center to prevent them from getting caught in stitching.*

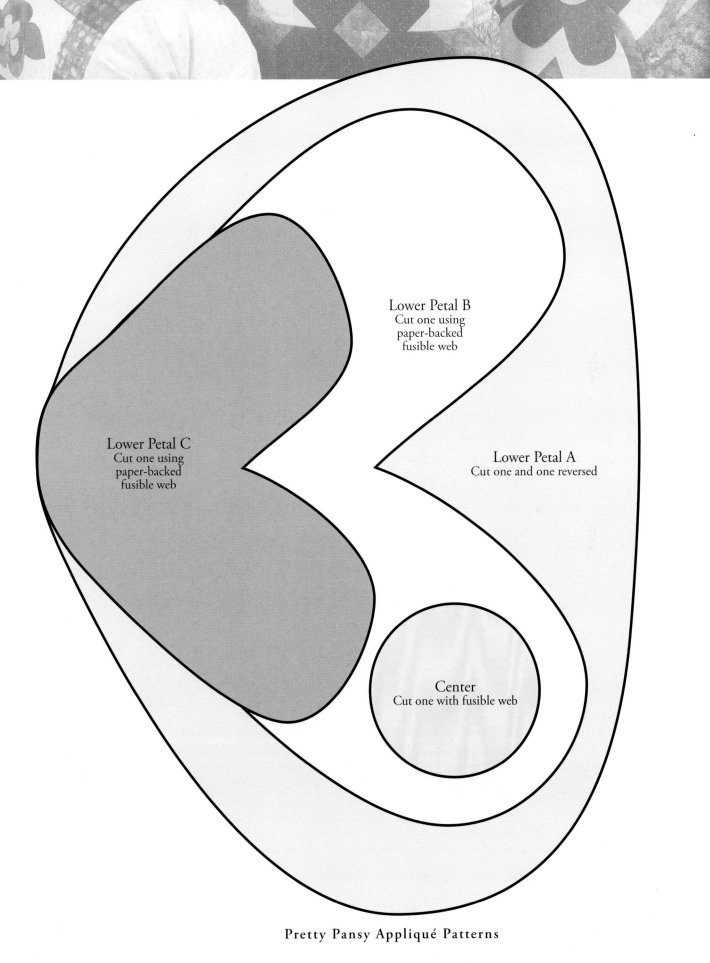

Lower Petal B
Cut one using
paper-backed
fusible web

Lower Petal C
Cut one using
paper-backed
fusible web

Lower Petal A
Cut one and one reversed

Center
Cut one with fusible web

Pretty Pansy Appliqué Patterns

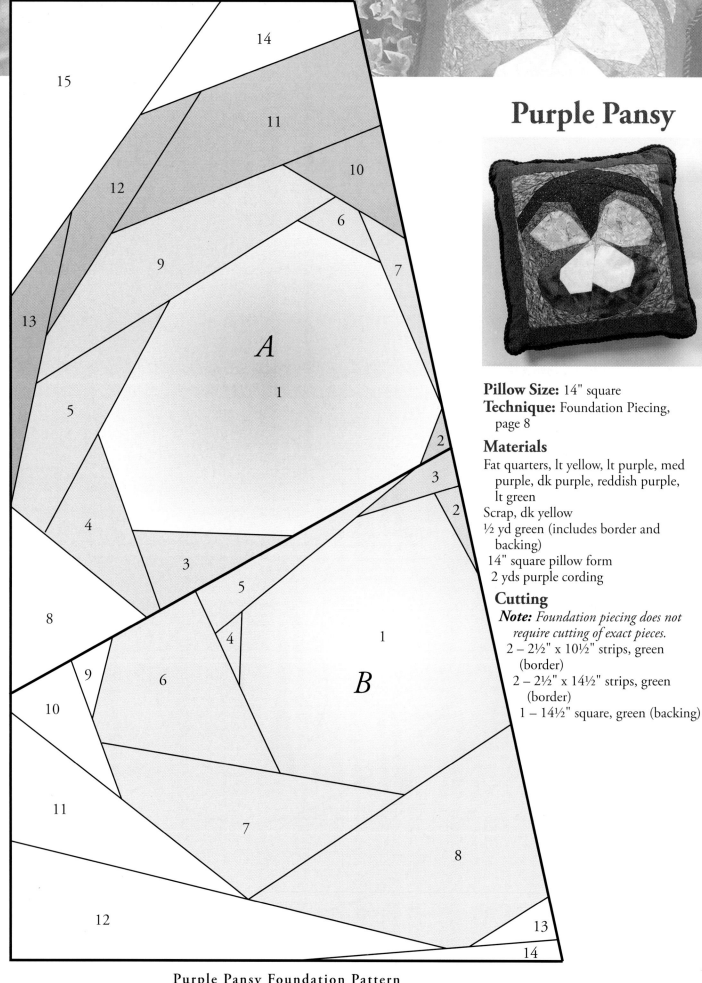

Purple Pansy

Pillow Size: 14" square
Technique: Foundation Piecing, page 8

Materials

Fat quarters, lt yellow, lt purple, med purple, dk purple, reddish purple, lt green
Scrap, dk yellow
½ yd green (includes border and backing)
14" square pillow form
2 yds purple cording

Cutting

Note: Foundation piecing does not require cutting of exact pieces.
2 – 2½" x 10½" strips, green (border)
2 – 2½" x 14½" strips, green (border)
1 – 14½" square, green (backing)

Purple Pansy Foundation Pattern

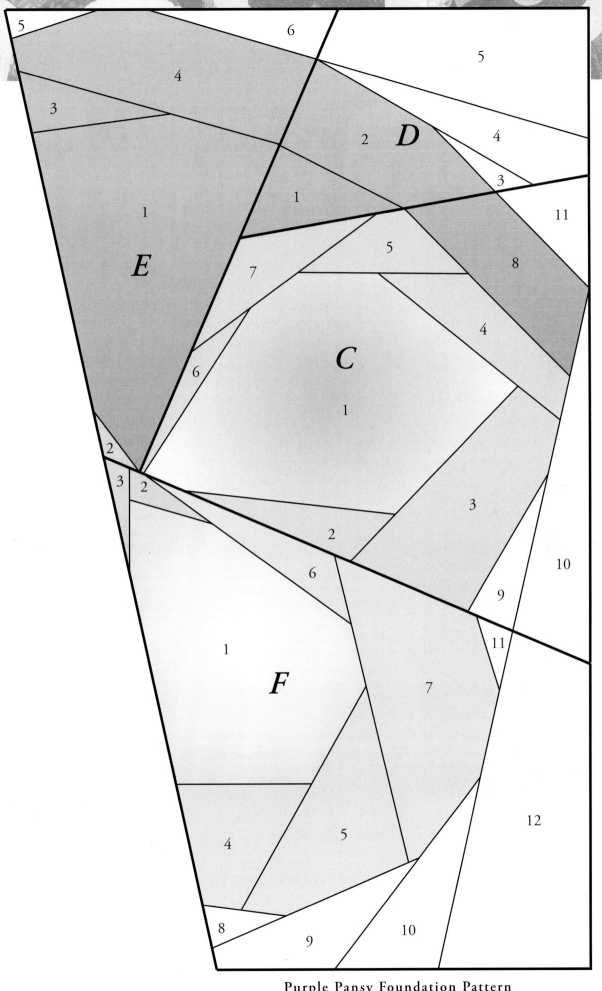

Purple Pansy Foundation Pattern

Instructions

1. Make Pansy referring to Foundation Piecing and using pattern on pages 50 and 51, **Fig 1**.

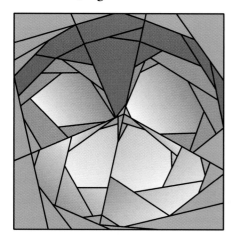

Fig 1

2. Sew 2½" x 10½" green strips to sides of block; press seams toward border. Sew 2½" x 14½" green strips to top and bottom, **Fig 2**; press seams toward border.

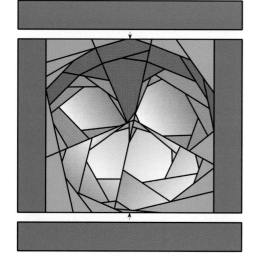

Fig 2

3. Remove paper foundations.

4. Refer to Pillows With Trimmed Edges, page 12, to finish pillow.

Pieced Pansy

Pillow Size: 14" square
Technique: Stitch & Flip, page 6

Materials
Fat quarters, green, white, lt purple, med purple, dk purple
Scrap, gold
Fat quarter, backing fabric
14" pillow form

Cutting
4 – 1¾" squares, gold (A)
2 – 4½" squares, dk purple (B)
2 – 3½" squares, dk purple (K)
4 – 1½" squares, med purple (C)
2 – 2¼" x 4½" strips, med purple (D)
2 – 2¼" x 6¼" strips, med purple (E)
2 – 2¼" squares, green (F)
2 – 1¾" squares, green (G)
2 – 1½" squares, green (H)
2 – 1¾" x 6¼" strips, green (I)
2 – 1¾" x 6¼" strips, green (J)
2 – 2¾" squares, green (S)
4 – 1¾" squares, green (T)
4 – 1½" squares, white (L)
2 – 2½" x 3½" strips, white (M)
2 – 2¼" x 5½" strips, white (N)
2 – 1¾" squares, lt purple (O)
4 – 1½" squares, lt purple (P)
2 – 2½" x 5¼" strips, lt purple (Q)
2 – 2 ¾" x 7½" strips, lt purple (R)
1 – 14½" square, backing fabric

Instructions

1. Using the stitch and flip technique throughout, sew an A square and two C squares to a B square, **Fig 23**.

Fig 23

2. Sew G square to D strip, noting placement, **Fig 24**.

3. Sew D/G strip to B/A/C square, **Fig 25**.

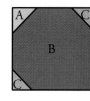

Fig 24

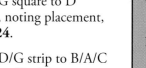

Fig 25

4. Sew F and H square to E strip noting placement, **Fig 26**.

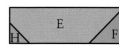

Fig 26

5. Sew E/F/H strip to adjacent side, **Fig 27**.

6. Attach I strip, then J strip to unit from step 5 to complete Lower block, **Fig 28**.

Fig. 27

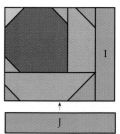

Fig 28

7. Repeat steps 1–6 for another Lower block.

8. Using stitch and flip technique, sew one A and two L squares to K square, **Fig 29**.

9. Sew P square to M strip, **Fig 30**.

Fig 29

Fig 30

10. Sew M/P strip to K/A/L square, **Fig 31**.

11. Sew O and P squares to N strip, **Fig 32**.

Fig 31   Fig 32

12. Sew N/O/P strip to adjacent side, **Fig 33**.

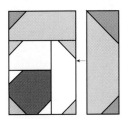

Fig 33

13. Using the stitch and flip method, sew T square to Q strip and S and T squares to R strip, noting positions, **Fig 34**.

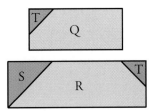

Fig 34

14. Attach Q strip, then R strip to unit from step 13 to complete Upper block, **Fig 35**.

Fig 35

15. Repeat steps 8–14 for another Upper block.

16. Sew upper blocks together; sew lower blocks together. Sew the pairs of blocks together to complete pillow top, **Fig 36.**

17. Refer to Basic Pillow, page 12, to finish pillow.

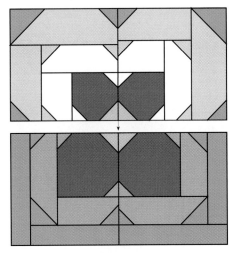

Fig 36

Nine-Patch Pansies

Pillow Size: 12" pillow plus 2" flange
Technique: Rotary Cutting, page 4

Materials
½ yd pansy print (includes border and backing)
Fat quarter, dk green
12" pillow form

Cutting
5 – 4½" squares, pansy print
4 – 4½" squares, dk green
2 – 2½" x 12½" strips, pansy print (flange)
2 – 2½" x 16½" strips, pansy print (flange)
1 – 16½" square, pansy print (backing)

Instructions

1. For rows 1 and 3, sew pansy print square to opposite sides of dk green, **Fig 37**; repeat.

Rows 1 & 3

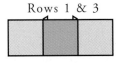

Fig 37

2. For row 2, sew dk green square to opposite sides of pansy print square, **Fig 38**.

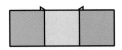

Fig 38

3. Sew rows of squares together to make Nine-Patch, **Fig 39**.

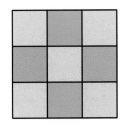

Fig 39

4. Sew 2½" x 12½" pansy print strips to sides of Nine-Patch; press seams toward strips. Sew 2½" x 16½" pansy print strips to top and bottom, **Fig 40**; press seams toward strips.

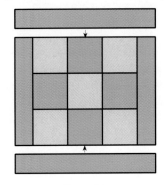

Fig 40

5. Refer to Pillows With a Flange, page 13, to finish pillow.

Rolling Pansies

2 – 2¾"-wide strips, dk purple
2 – 2¾"-wide strips, dk green
2 – 6" x 27½" rectangles, lt background

Instructions

1. Referring to **Fig 13,** fuse Leaves, Upper Petals A, B and C, Lower Petals A and B and Center to 5" x 9½"lt background rectangle. Machine-zigzag around each shape if desired.

2. Sew dk purple and dk green 2¾"-wide strips together lengthwise, **Fig 14**. Press seams toward purple.

3. Cut strips at 2¾" intervals to form pairs of squares, **Fig 15**.

Fig 14

Pillow Size: 14" x 9" neck-roll pillow
Technique: Easy Machine Appliqué, page 7

Materials

Fat quarters, lt background, yellow, lt purple, dk purple, med purple, green Scrap, gold
¼ yd dk purple (checkerboard)
¼ yd dk green (checkerboard)
9" x 14" neck-roll pillow form
2 – 1⅜" gold filigree buttons
½ yd paper-backed fusible web

Cutting

Note: *See Easy Machine Appliqué to cut out patterns found below with paper-backed fusible web.*

6 – Leaves, green
3 – Lower Petal A, med purple
3 – Lower Petal B, yellow
3 – Upper Petal-Right A, lt purple
3 – Upper Petal-Right B, dk purple
3 – Upper Petal-Right C, yellow
3 – Upper Petal-Left A, lt purple
3 – Upper Petal-Left B, dk purple
3 – Upper Petal-Left C, yellow
3 – Center, gold
3 – 5" x 9½" rectangles, lt background

Fig 13

Fig 15

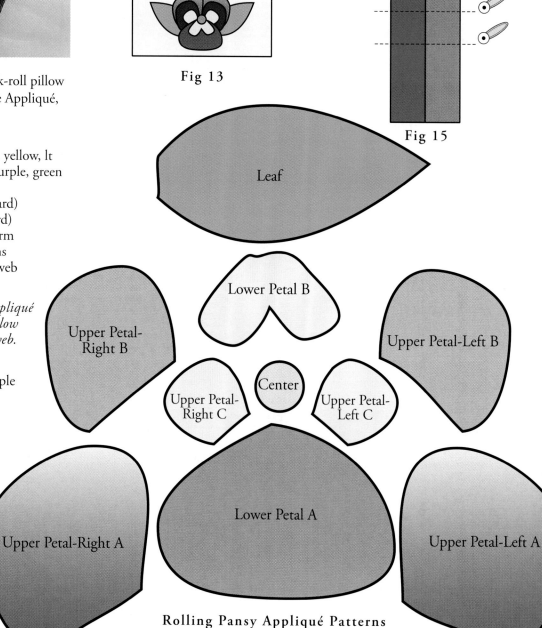

Leaf

Lower Petal B

Upper Petal-Right B

Upper Petal-Left B

Upper Petal-Right C

Center

Upper Petal-Left C

Upper Petal-Right A

Lower Petal A

Upper Petal-Left A

Rolling Pansy Appliqué Patterns

4. Sew pairs of squares together, **Fig 16**. Repeat five more times.

Fig 16

5. Sew strips from step 4 to top and bottom edges of each pansy rectangle, noting position of green and purple squares, **Fig 17**.

Fig 17

6. Sew pansy rectangles together, **Fig 18**.

Fig 18

7. Sew six pairs of squares together; repeat, **Fig 19**.

Fig 19

8. Sew squares to sides of pansies, **Fig 20**.

Fig 20

9. Sew 6" x 27½" rectangle to each side to complete pillow top, **Fig 21**.

Fig 21

10. Fold pillow top in half crosswise with right sides together; sew along longest edge to form a tube, **Fig 22**.

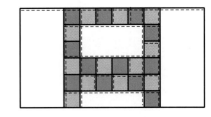

Fig 22

11. For sides, fold raw edges under ¼"; sew along fold.

12. Turn tube right side out and place pillow form through openings. Neatly fold ends toward center; tack in place. Sew 1⅜" gold filigree buttons in center to finish pillow.

Playful Snowmen

This playful group of snowmen pillows will be the perfect accent to your winter or holiday decor.

Snowman Family

Pillow Size: 12" x 16"
Technique: Easy Machine Appliqué, page 7

Materials

⅛ yd white polar fleece
Fat quarter, white
Scraps, green, red, brown
½ yd blue (includes backing)
3 small red beads
3 small blue beads
9 small black beads
6 small black bugle beads
12" x 16" pillow form
1 yd paper-backed fusible web such as Thermoweb's HeatnBond UltraHold (If you are going to machine-stitch around shapes, you will need to use HeatnBond Lite.)
Washable craft glue such as Aleene's Jewel-It
Optional: *Black permanent marker*

Cutting

Note: *See Easy Machine Appliqué, page 7, to cut out patterns found on page 57, 58, 59 and 61.*

1 – Snowman 1, polar fleece
1 – Snowman 2, polar fleece

1 – Snowman 3, polar fleece
1 – Large Tree Snow, polar fleece
1 – Small Tree Snow, polar fleece
1 – Large Tree, green
1 – Small Tree, green
1 – Large Tree Trunk, brown
1 – Small Tree Trunk, brown
1 – Hat 1, red
1 – Vest, red
1 – Hat 2, green
1 – Scarf, green
1 – Hat 3, green
1 – 8½" x 16½" rectangle, white
2 – 12½" x 16½" rectangles, blue

Instructions

1. Cut a slightly wavy edge along one long side of white rectangle, **Fig 1**. Fuse to right side of one of the blue rectangles, **Fig 2**.

Fig 1

Fig 2

Cut wavy line

2. Position Large Tree and Snow, Small Tree and Snow, and three Snowmen on snowy background, **Fig 3**; fuse in place. **Note:** *Use machine zigzag and invisible thread to stitch along edges of shapes if desired.*

Fig 3

3. Sew or glue beads in place on Snowmen referring to photograph. **Optional:** *Draw mouths with black permanent marker.*

4. Refer to Basic Pillow, page 12, to finish pillow.

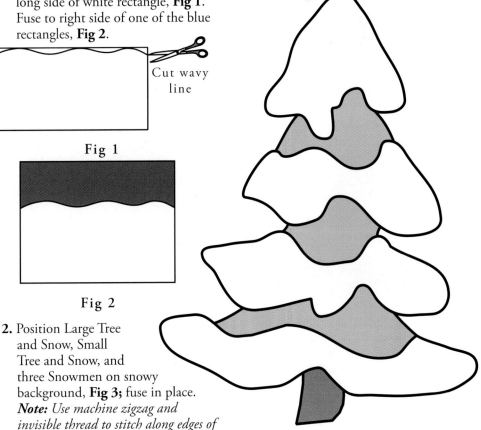

Small Tree

Lone Snowman

Pillow Size: 14" square plus 2" flange
Technique: Easy Machine Appliqué, page 7

Materials

⅛ yd white polar fleece
Fat quarter, white
Scraps, green, red, brown
½ yd blue (includes backing)
Fat quarter, blue print
14" pillow form
Three small black beads
Three small black bugle beads
1 yd paper-backed heavy-duty fusible web such as Thermoweb's HeatnBond UltraHold
Optional: Black permanent marker

Cutting

Note: *See Easy Machine Appliqué, page 7, to cut out patterns found on page 57 and 58.*

1 – Snowman 1, white polar fleece
1 – Hat 1, red
1 – Vest, red
4 – Small Tree, green
4 – Small Tree Trunk, brown
1 – 9½" x 14½" rectangle, white
1 – 14½" x 14½" square, blue
2 – 2½" x 14½" strips, blue
2 – 2½" x 18½" strips, blue

Instructions

1. Cut a slightly wavy edge along one side of white rectangle, **Fig 4**. Remove paper and fuse to blue background square, **Fig 5**.

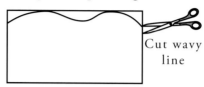

Cut wavy line

Fig 4

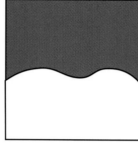

Fig 5

2. Position Small Trees and Snowman 1 on snowy background referring to **Fig 6**; fuse in place. ***Note:*** *Use machine zigzag and invisible thread to stitch along edges of shapes if desired.*

Fig 6

3. Sew or glue small black beads and bugle beads on snowman face. ***Optional:*** *Draw mouth with permanent black marker.*

4. Sew 2½" x 14½" blue strips to sides of pillow top; sew 2½" x 18½" strips to top and bottom, **Fig 7**.

Fig 7

5. Refer to Pillows With a Flange, page 13, to finish pillow.

Snowman 1

Caught in a Snowstorm

Pillow Size: 12" square plus 2" flange
Technique: Easy Appliqué, page 7

Materials

⅛ yd white polar fleece
Fat quarter, white
Scraps, red, green, brown
⅝ yd blue (includes backing and flange)
1 yd white floral trim (for snowflakes)
Several ¼" small white buttons
10 small black beads
3 small blue beads
3 small black bugle beads
12" square pillow form
1 yd paper-backed heavy-duty fusible
    web such as Thermoweb's HeatnBond
    UltraHold
Optional: Black permanent marker

Cutting

*Note: See Easy Appliqué, to cut out
patterns found on page 59 and 61.*

1 – Snowman 1, white polar fleece
1 – Snowman 3, white polar fleece
1 – Large Tree Snow, white polar fleece
1 – Large Tree, green
1 – Large Tree Trunk, brown
1 – Hat 2, green
1 – Hat 3, red
1 – Scarf, green
1 – 12½" x 8" rectangle, white
1 – 12½" square, blue
1 – 16½" square, blue (backing)
2 – 2½" x 12½" strips, blue
2 – 2½" x 16½" strips, blue

Instructions

1. Cut a slightly wavy edge along one
   side of white square, **Fig 8**. Remove
   paper and fuse to blue background
   square, **Fig 9**.

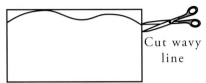

Cut wavy
line

Fig 8

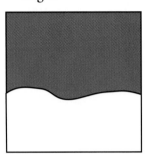

Fig 9

2. Position Large Tree, Snowman
   2 and Snowman 3 on
   snowy background,
   Fig 10; fuse in
   place. ***Note:*** *Use
   machine zigzag
   and invisible
   thread to
   stitch
   along
   edges of
   shapes if
   desired.*

Fig 10

3. Sew or glue small beads and
   bugle beads on snowmen.
   *Optional: Draw mouths with black
   permanent marker.*

4. Cut individual flowers from trim.
   Sew or glue randomly on background;
   don't place too close to edges.

5. Sew 2½" x 14½" blue strips to sides
   of pillow top; sew 2½" x 18½" blue
   strips to top and bottom, **Fig 11**.

Fig 11

6. Refer to Pillows With a Flange, page
   13, to finish pillow.

7. Sew or glue flowers randomly on
   flange.

Snowman 2

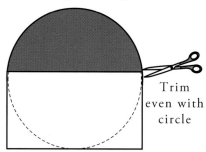

Snowmen in the Round

Pillow Size: 12" round
Technique: Easy Machine Appliqué, page 7

Materials
⅛ yd white polar fleece
Fat quarter, white
Scraps, red, green, brown
½ yd blue (includes backing)
1½ yds white fringe trim
12" round pillow form
9 – small dark beads
6 – small bugle beads
3 – green beads
3 – red beads
Optional: Black permanent marker

Cutting
Note: See Easy Machine Appliqué, page 7, to cut out patterns found on pages 57, 58, 59 and 61.

1 – Snowman 1, white polar fleece
1 – Snowman 2, white polar fleece
1 – Snowman 3, white polar fleece
1 – Small Tree Snow, white polar fleece
1 – Small Tree, green
1 – Small Tree Trunk, brown
1 – Hat 1, green
1 – Vest, green
1 – Hat 2, red
1 – Scarf, red
1 – Hat 3, green
1 – 12½" x 8" rectangle, white
2 – 12½" circles, blue

Instructions
1. Pin white rectangle to one blue background circle and trim white fabric even with curved blue edge, **Fig 12**. Remove paper and fuse to blue background, **Fig 13**.

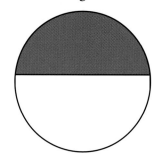

Trim even with circle

Fig 12

Fig 13

2. Position Small Tree and Snowman 1, 2 and 3 on snowy background referring to **Fig 14**; fuse in place. *Note: Use machine zigzag and invisible thread to stitch along edges of shapes if desired.*

Fig 14

3. Sew or glue beads on Snowmen's faces and bodies. *Optional: Draw mouth with permanent black marker.*

4. Refer to Pillows With Trimmed Edges, page 12, to finish pillow.

Where are the Snowmen?

Pillow Size: 14" square
Technique: Easy Machine Appliqué, page 7

Materials
⅛ yd white polar fleece
Fat quarter, white
Scraps, brown
½ yd blue (includes backing)
2 yds pompom trim
Several small white buttons
1 strand of miniature Christmas bulbs
14" pillow form

Cutting
1 – Large Tree Snow, polar fleece
3 – Small Tree Snow, polar fleece
1 – Large Tree, green
3 – Small Tree, green
1 – Large Tree Trunk, brown
3 – Small Tree Trunk, brown
1 – 14½" x 8" rectangle, white
2 – 14½" squares, blue

Instructions
1. Cut a slightly wavy edge along one side of white rectangle, **Fig 15**. Remove paper and fuse to blue background, **Fig 16**.

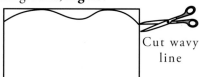

Cut wavy line

Fig 15

2. Position Small Trees and Large Tree on snowy background referring to **Fig 17**; fuse in place. ***Note:*** *Use machine zigzag and invisible thread to stitch along edges of shapes if desired.*

Fig 16

Fig 17

Snowman 3

3. Sew or glue white buttons on blue background. Sew or glue miniature Christmas bulbs on trees.

4. Refer to Pillows With Trimmed Edges, page 12, to finish pillow.

Large Tree

VISIONS
ANGELS
an Photographers share their images

Angels Around Us

This heavenly collection of pillows will add a sense of warmth and joy to any home. Whether you like to do appliqué, foundation piecing or just patchwork, you will find an angel pillow to make.

Guardian Angel

Pillow Size: 16" square
Technique: Foundation Piecing, pages 8 to 11

Materials

Fat quarters, white, med blue, blue floral print, lt blue, med pink
Scraps, peach (skin color), brown (hair color)
Fat quarter backing
16" pillow form
2 yds ruffle trim

Cutting

Note: *Foundation Piecing does not require exact cutting of pieces.*

2 – 1½" x 10½" strips, med pink (first border)
2 – 1½" x 12½" strips, med pink (first border)
2 – 2½" x 12½" strips, blue floral print (second border)
2 – 2½" x 16½" strips, blue floral print (second border)
1 – 16½" square, backing fabric

Instructions

1. Referring to Foundation Piecing, make Guardian Angel block using patterns on pages 64 and 65, **Fig 1**.

2. Sew 1½" x 10½" med pink strips to opposite sides of Angel; sew 1½" x 12½" med pink strips to top and bottom. Sew 2½" x 12½" blue floral print strips to opposite sides of Angel; sew 2½" x 16½" blue floral print strips to top and bottom, **Fig 2**.

3. Refer to Pillows With Trimmed Edges, page 12, to finish pillow.

Fig 1

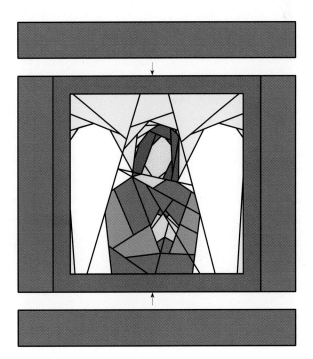

Fig 2

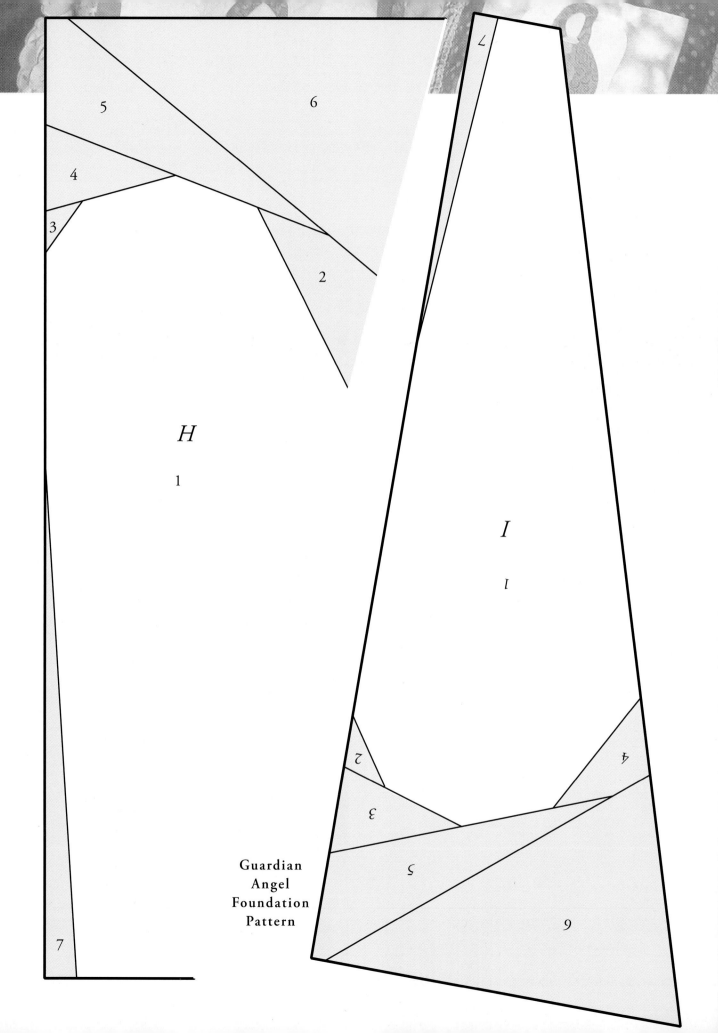

5

6

4

3

2

H

1

I

1

7

5

2

3

4

5

6

7

Guardian
Angel
Foundation
Pattern

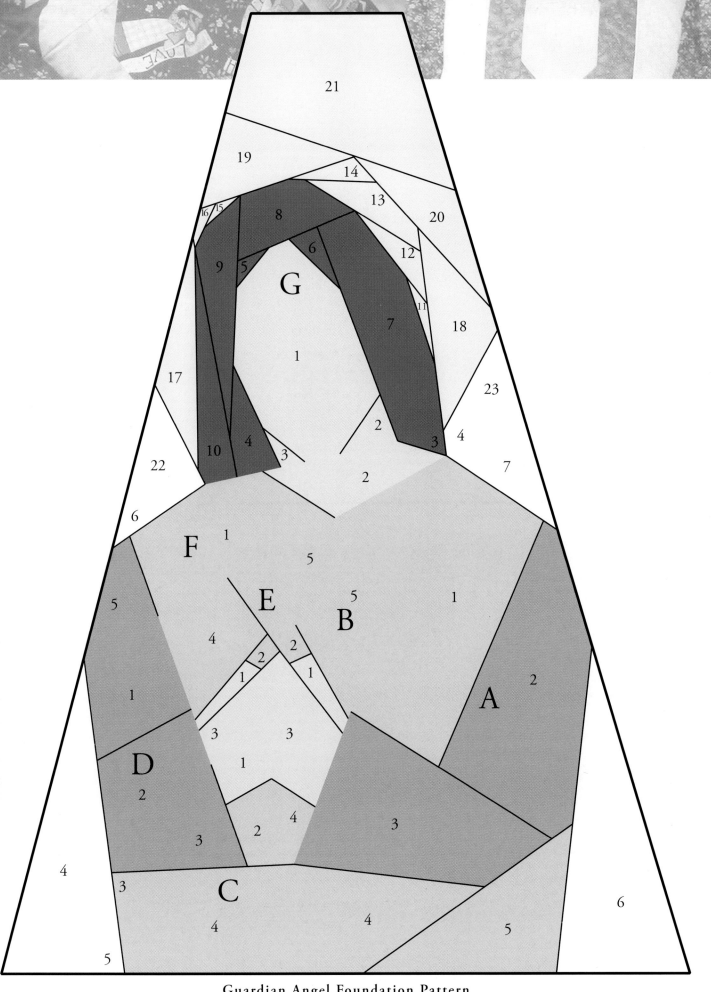

Guardian Angel Foundation Pattern

Prayerful Angel

Pillow Size: 12" x 16"
Technique: Easy Machine Appliqué, page 8

Materials

Fat quarters, lt blue, blue/purple, purple, cream
Scraps, peach (skin color), brown (hair color)
½ yd dk blue (border and backing)
12" x 16" pillow form
2 yds tassel fringe trim
1 yd paper-backed fusible web

Cutting

Note: *See Easy Machine Appliqué to cut out patterns on page 67.*

1 Dress Front, blue/purple
1 Dress Side and one reversed, purple
1 Sleeves, purple
1 Wing and one reversed, cream
1 Neck, peach
1 Face, peach
1 Hands, peach
1 Hair, brown
1 – 8½" x 12½" rectangle, lt blue
4 – 2½" x 12½" strips, dk blue
1 – 12½" x 16½" rectangle, dk blue

Instructions

1. Following manufacturer's directions, fuse angel to lt blue background rectangle referring to **Fig 3**. Machine-zigzag around each shape if desired.

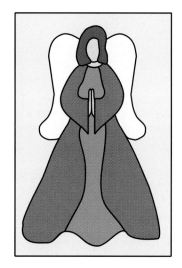

Fig 3

2. Sew 2½" x 12½" dk blue strips to sides first, then to top and bottom, **Fig 4**.

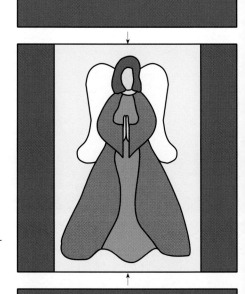

Fig 4

3. Refer to Pillows With Trimmed Edges, page 12, to finish pillow.

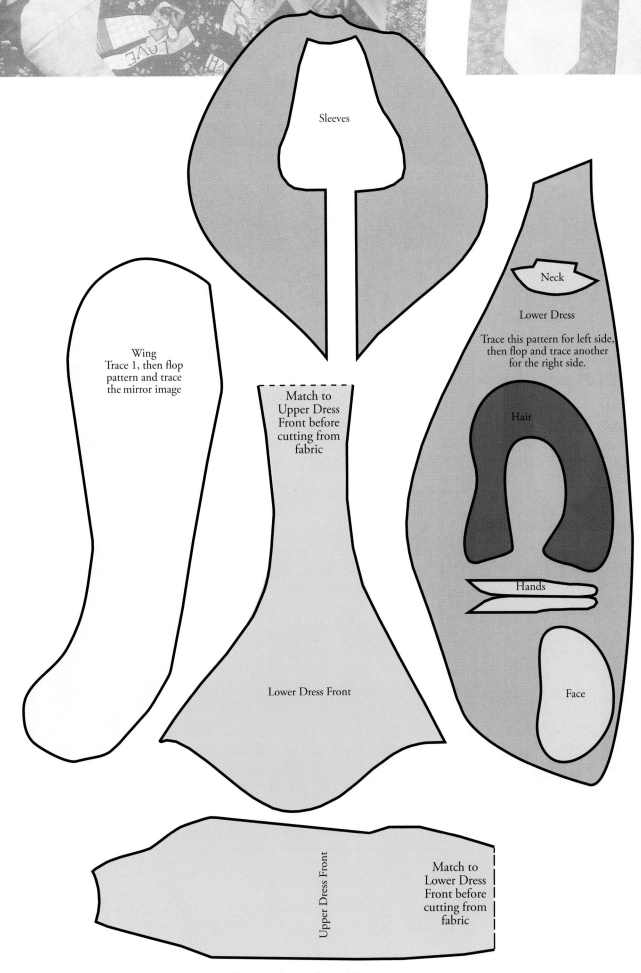

Sleeves

Wing
Trace 1, then flop
pattern and trace
the mirror image

Neck

Lower Dress

Trace this pattern for left side,
then flop and trace another
for the right side.

Hair

Hands

Face

Match to
Upper Dress
Front before
cutting from
fabric

Lower Dress Front

Upper Dress Front

Match to
Lower Dress
Front before
cutting from
fabric

Prayerful Angel Appliqué Patterns

Framed Angels

Pillow Size: 14" square
Technique: Stitch & Flip, page 6

Materials
½ yd angel print (includes flange and backing)
Scraps, dk blue
10" square, lavender
14" pillow form

Cutting
1 – 9" square, angel print
2 – 3¼" x 9" strips, lavender
2 – 3¼" x 14½" strips, lavender
4 – 2¼" squares, lavender
4 – 3¼" squares, dk blue
2 – 2½" x 14½" strips, angel print (flange)
2 – 2½" x 18½" strips, angel print (flange)

Instructions

1. Using the stitch and flip method, sew 2¼" lavender square to each corner of angel print square, **Fig 21**.

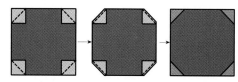

Fig 21

2. Sew 3¼" x 9" lavender strips to sides of angel print square; sew 3¼" x 14½" strips to top and bottom, **Fig 22**.

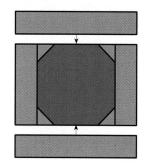

Fig 22

3. Using the stitch and flip method, sew 3¼" dk blue square to each corner, **Fig 23**.

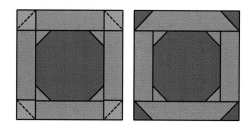

Fig 23

4. Sew 2½" x 14½" angel print strips to sides and 2½" x 18½" angel print strips to top and bottom, **Fig 24**.

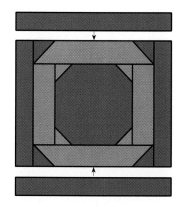

Fig 24

5. Refer to Pillows With a Flange, page 13, to finish pillow.

Pieceful Angel

Pillow Size: 12" square plus 2" flange
Technique: Stitch & Flip, page 6

Materials
Fat quarter, white, lt blue
Scraps, peach (skin), brown (hair)
½ yd dk blue print (flange and backing)
12" square pillow form

Cutting
4 – 3½" squares, white (A)
2 – 2" x 3½" rectangles, white (B)
4 – 2" squares, white (C)
2 – 3½" x 5" rectangles, white (D)
1 – 3½" x 5" rectangles, peach (E)
4 – 2" squares, dk blue (F)
1 – 2" x 6½" rectangle, brown (G)
4 – 1¼" squares, brown (H)
2 – 2" x 5" rectangles, brown (I)
2 – 2" squares, brown (J)
1 – 5" x 6½" rectangles, lt blue (K)
6 – 2" squares, lt blue (L)
2 – 2½" x 12½" strips, dk blue print
2 – 2½" x 16½" strips, dk blue print
1 – 16½" square, backing fabric

Instructions
Row 1
1. Using the stitch and flip method, sew an F square to an A square, **Fig 5**; repeat.

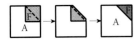

Fig 5

2. Using the stitch and flip method, sew a C square to each end of a G rectangle, **Fig 6**.

Fig 6

3. Using the stitch and flip method, sew an F square to a B rectangle; repeat with F square at other end of B to make a mirror image, **Fig 7**.

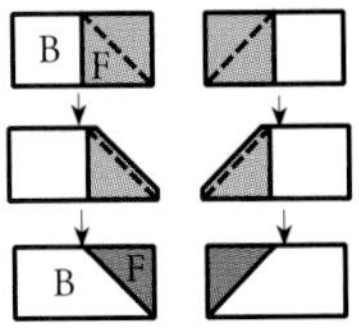

Fig 7

4. Sew units from steps 2 and 3 together, **Fig 8**.

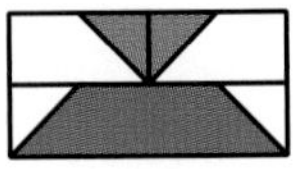

Fig 8

5. Sew units from steps 1 and 4 together to finish row 1, **Fig 9**.

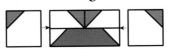

Fig 9

Row 2
6. Using the stitch and flip method, sew an H square to all four corners of E rectangle, **Fig 10**.

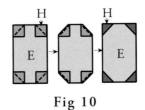

Fig 10

7. Sew an I rectangle to opposite sides of unit from step 6, **Fig 11**.

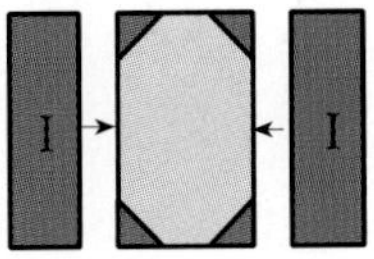

Fig 11

8. Sew a D rectangle to I rectangles to complete row 2, **Fig 12**.

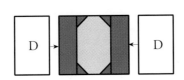

Fig 12

Row 3
9. Using the stitch and flip method, sew J squares to upper corners of K rectangle and L squares to lower corners, **Fig 13**.

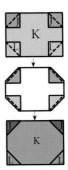

Fig 13

10. Using the stitch and flip method, sew an L square to A square, **Fig 14**; repeat.

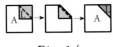

Fig 14

11. Sew an L square to a C square, **Fig 15**; repeat.

Fig 15

12. Sew units from steps 10 and 11 together; be sure they are mirror images, **Fig 16**.

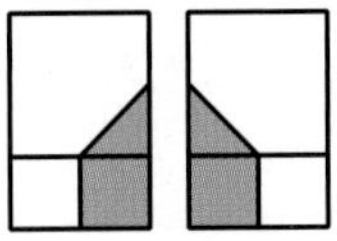

Fig 16

13. Sew units from step 12 to unit from step 9 to complete row 3, **Fig 17**.

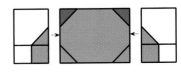

Fig 17

Finishing

14. Sew rows 1, 2 and 3 together to complete block, **Fig 18**.

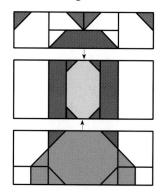

Fig 18

15. Sew 2½" x 12½" dk blue print strips to sides of block; sew 2½" x 16½" dk blue print strips to top and bottom, **Fig 19**.

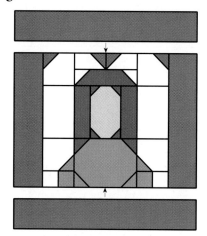

Fig 19

16. Refer to Pillows With a Flange, page 13, to finish pillow.

Angel Round

Pillow Size: 12" round
Technique: Easy Machine Appliqué, page 7

Materials

Scraps, cream, peach (skin), brown (hair), purple, purple/blue
½ yd med blue background (includes backing)
1½ yds cording
1 yd paper-backed fusible web

Cutting

Note: *See Easy Machine Appliqué to cut out patterns found on pages 72 and 73.*

1 Dress Center, purple/blue
1 Dress Sides, purple
1 Neck, peach
1 Face, peach
1 Hair, brown
1 Wing and 1 Wing reverse, cream
1 – 12½" circle, med blue background fabric

Instructions

1. Following manufacturer's directions, fuse angel pieces to background circle referring to **Fig 20**. Machine-zigzag around each shape if desired.

2. Refer to Pillows With Trimmed Edges, page 12, to finish pillow.

Fig 20

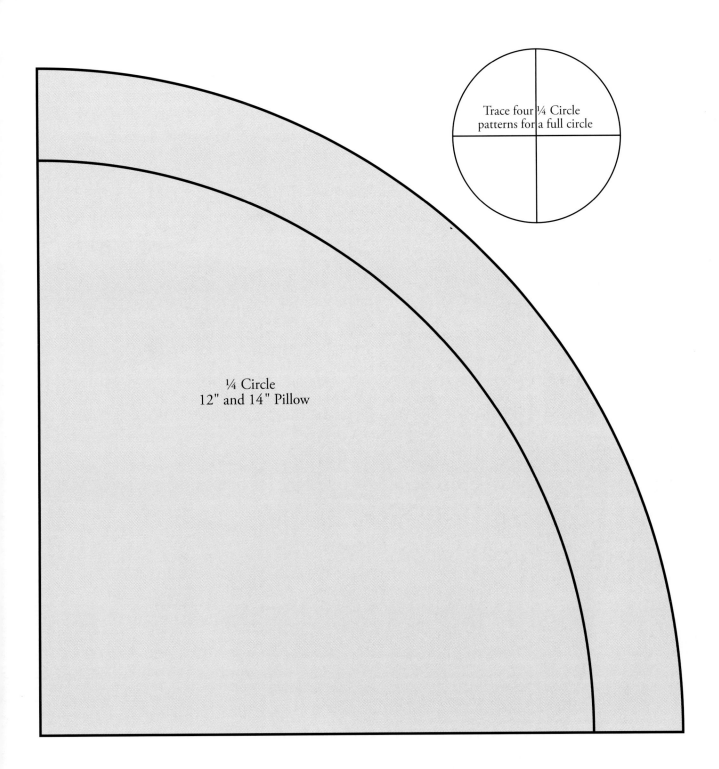

Trace four ¼ Circle
patterns for a full circle

¼ Circle
12" and 14" Pillow

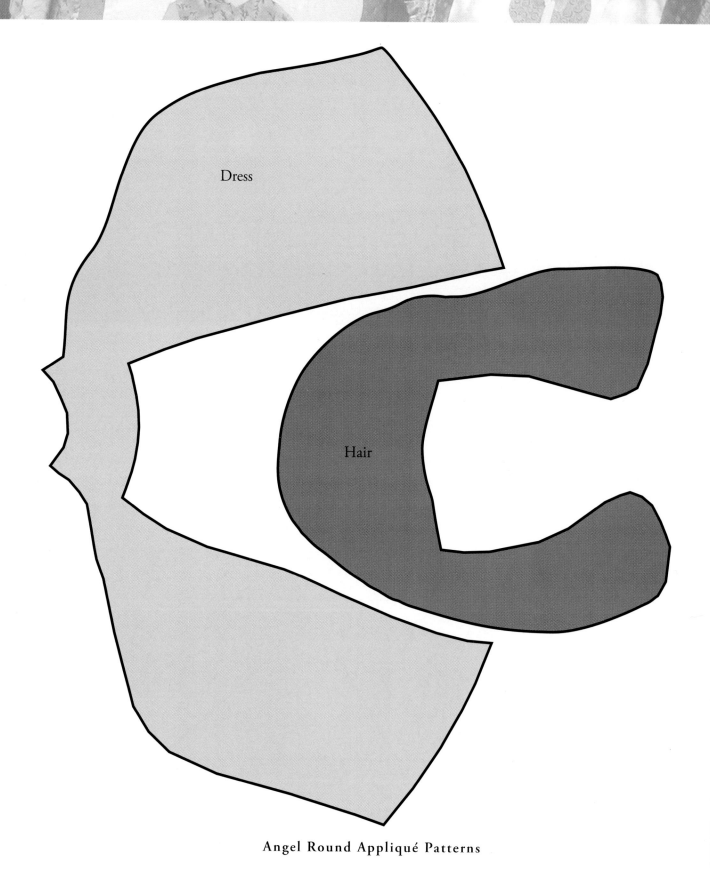

Dress

Hair

Angel Round Appliqué Patterns

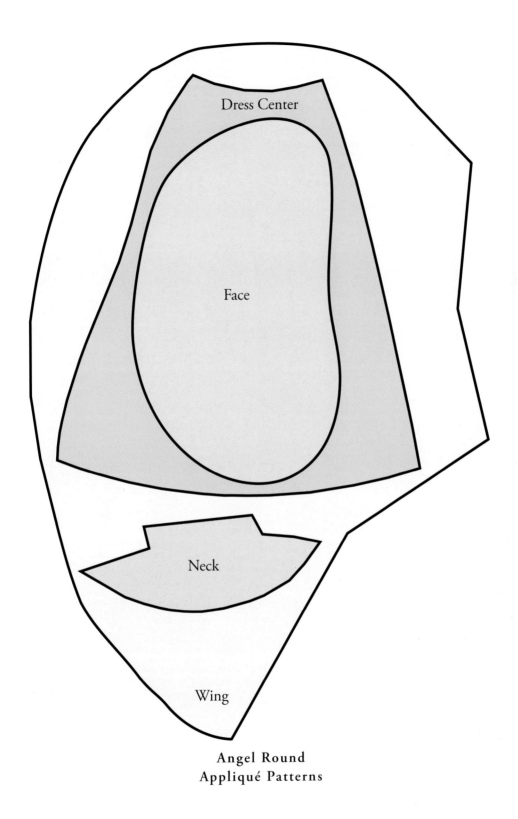

Dress Center

Face

Neck

Wing

Angel Round
Appliqué Patterns

Sunny Flowers

The colorful floral pillows in this group are sure to bring a little sunshine to any room in your home.

Floral Picture

Pillow Size: 12" square plus 2"-wide flange

Technique: Stitch & Flip, page 6

Materials

½ yd floral print (includes backing)
Fat quarter, red
¼ yd gold
12" pillow form

Cutting

1 – 12½" square, floral
2 – 6½" squares, red
2 – 2½" x 12½" strips, gold
2 – 2½" x 16½" strips, gold
1 – 16½" square, backing

Instructions

1. Draw diagonal line on wrong side of red squares.

2. Using stitch and flip method, sew a red square to a floral square along drawn line, **Fig 1**.

Fig 1

3. Cut ¼" from drawn line and flip triangle over, **Fig 2**.

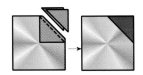

Fig 2

4. Repeat at remaining corners, **Fig 3**.

Fig 3

5. Sew 2½" x 12½" gold strips to sides of block; press seams toward strips. Sew 2½" x 16½" gold strips to top and bottom, **Fig 4**; press seams toward strips.

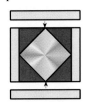

Fig 4

6. Refer to Pillows With a Flange, page 13, to finish pillow.

Flower Planter Flap

Pillow Size: 14" square

Technique: Rotary Cutting, page 4

Materials

Fat quarters, med green, dk green, red, gold
½ yd floral print (includes backing)
14" pillow form

Cutting

1 – 2½" x 8½" strip, red
2 – 2" x 2½" strips, med green
2 – 2" x 5" strips, med green
2 – 1¾" x 11½" strips, dk green
2 – 1¾" x 14½" strips, dk green
2 – 7½" x 14½" rectangles, floral
2 – 7½" x 14½" rectangle, gold

Instructions

1. Sew 2" x 2½" med green strip to 2½" x 8½" red strip, **Fig 5**. Press seams to one side.

Fig 5

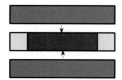

2. Sew 1¾" x 11½" dk green strips to top and bottom, **Fig 6**. Press seams to one side.

Fig 6

3. Sew 2" x 5" med green strips to sides, **Fig 7**. Press seams to one side.

Fig 7

4. Sew 1¾" x 14½" dk green strips to top and bottom to finish block, **Fig 8**. Press seams to one side.

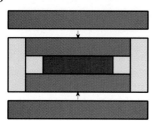

Fig 8

5. Sew block to 7½" x 14½" gold rectangle, **Fig 9**.

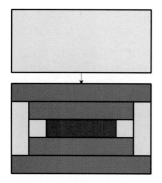

Fig 9

6. Refer to Pillows With a Flap, page 13, to finish pillow.

Flower Basket

Pillow size: 14" square plus 2"-wide flange
Technique: Rotary Cutting, page 4

Materials

Fat quarters, floral print, plaid, very lt blue
⅝ yd red (flange and backing)
14" pillow form

Cutting

2 – 2½" x 3½" rectangles, very lt blue
2 – 2½" squares, very lt blue
2 – 5½" squares, very lt blue
1 – 8" square cut in half diagonally, very lt blue
1 – 2½" x 8½" rectangle, plaid
1 – 5½" x 14½" rectangle, plaid
1 – 2" x 9¼" rectangle, plaid
1 – 2" x 10¾" rectangle, plaid
1 – 7¾" square cut in half diagonally, floral
2 – 2½" x 14½" strips, red (flange)
2 – 2½" x 18½" strips, red (flange)
1 – 18½" square, backing

Instructions

1. Using stitch and flip method, sew 2½" very lt blue squares to opposite sides of 2½" x 8½" plaid rectangle, **Fig 10**. Sew 2½" x 3½" very lt blue rectangle to each end, **Fig 11**.

Fig 10

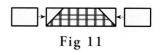

Fig 11

2. Using stitch and flip method, sew a 5½" very lt blue square to opposite sides of 5½" x 14½" plaid rectangle, **Fig 12**. Sew to strip from step 1, **Fig 13**.

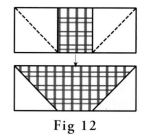

Fig 12

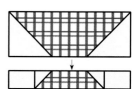

Fig 13

3. Sew 2" x 9¼" plaid rectangle to floral triangle, **Fig 14**; press seam toward

Fig 14

rectangle. Sew 2" x 10¾" plaid rectangle to adjacent side of floral rectangle, **Fig 15**. Trim strips even with edge of floral triangle, **Fig 16**. Sew a very lt blue triangle to opposite sides, **Fig 17**.

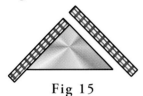

Fig 15

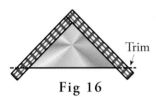

Fig 16

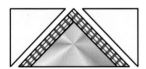

Fig 17

4. Sew floral and plaid sections together to complete basket, **Fig 18**.

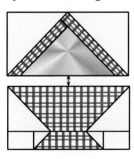

Fig 18

5. Sew 2½" x 14½" red strips to sides of basket; sew 2½" x 18" red strips to top and bottom.

6. Refer to Pillows With a Flange, page 13, to complete pillow.

Sunflower

Pillow Size: 14" round
Technique: Foundation Piecing, page 8.

Materials
½ yd yellow
Fat quarters, brown, dk green
½ yd lt green (includes backing)
14" round pillow form
2 yds cording

Cutting
Note: Foundation piecing does not require cutting exact pieces. Use patterns on pages 71 and 78 to make Flower Center and backing.

1 Flower Center, brown
1 – 14½" Circle, backing

Instructions
1. Make four Sunflower sections referring to Foundation Piecing and using pattern on page 78, **Fig 19**. *Note: Cut pattern out along inner and outer curved lines.*

Fig 19

2. Sew sections together in pairs, then sew pairs together, **Fig 20**.

Fig 20

3. Remove paper foundation.

4. Trace Flower Center quarter circle onto template plastic; cut out. Trace pattern four times onto wrong side of brown fabric to form a circle, **Fig 21**. Cut out circle ¼"–½" from drawn line.

Fig 21

5. Press outside edge of Flower Center under ¼" and place in center of flower petals, **Fig 22**. Machine-zigzag along edge of center using matching or invisible thread.

Fig 22

6. Refer to Pillows With Trimmed Edges, page 12, to finish pillow.

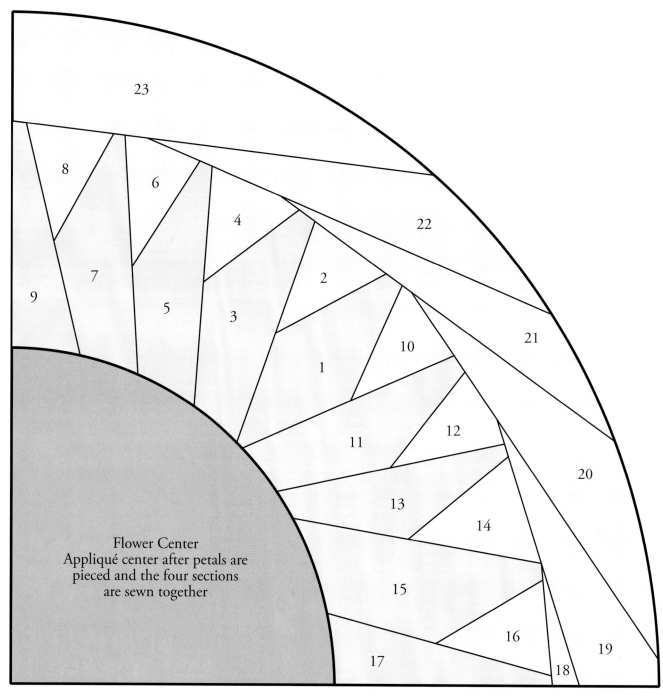

23

8

6

4

22

7

9

2

21

5

3

10

1

12

11

20

13

Flower Center
Appliqué center after petals are
pieced and the four sections
are sewn together

14

15

16

19

17

18

Sunflower Foundation Pattern

Sunny Sunflower

Pillow Size: 14" round

Technique: Easy Machine Appliqué,
page 7

Materials

½ yd yellow
Fat quarter, brown
½ yd green
14" round pillow form

Cutting

Note: *Refer to Easy Machine Appliqué, to cut the following shapes. The 14½" Circle pattern can be found on page 71.*

17 Petal, yellow
17 Petal (reversed), yellow
1 – Flower Center, brown
2 – 14½" Circle, green (one will be
   backing)

Instructions

1. Place a yellow Petal and a reversed yellow Petal, right sides together. Sew together entire edge except bottom edge, **Fig 23**. Repeat for remaining Petals.

Fig 23

2. Turn Petals right side out and press.

3. Arrange Petals evenly on background circle, **Fig 24**. Pin each in place.

Fig 24

4. Press edge of Flower Center under ¼". Place in center of Petals on background, **Fig 25**; pin in place.

Fig 25

5. Using machine zigzag and matching or invisible thread, sew around entire circle, not catching Petals in sewing.

6. Tack Petals to background if desired to keep them in place.

7. Refer to Basic Pillow, page 12, to finish pillow.

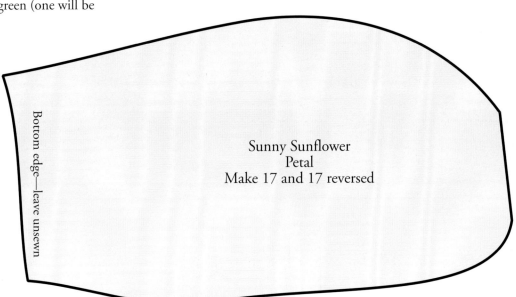

Bottom edge—leave unsewn

Sunny Sunflower
Petal
Make 17 and 17 reversed

Oriental Modern

In this group of pillows, Japanese Fish, Oriental Fan and Chinese Puzzle
are among the blocks that will bring an Eastern flavor to your decor.

Chinese Letters

Pillow Size: 12" square
Technique: Stitch & Flip, page 6

Materials
Fat quarters, black Oriental print, green print, blue print
Fat quarter, backing
12" pillow form

Cutting
1 – 8½" square, black Oriental print
4 – 2½" x 8½" rectangles, blue print
4 – 6½" squares, green print
1 – 12½" square, backing fabric

Instructions
1. Sew 2½" x 8½" blue print rectangle to each side of 8½" black Oriental print square, **Fig 1**.

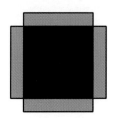

Fig 1

2. Draw diagonal line on wrong side of green print squares. Place green print square right sides together with unit from step 1 and sew along drawn line, **Fig 2**.

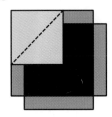

Fig 2

3. Trim ¼" from sewing line, **Fig 3**.

4. Flip triangle over; press, **Fig 4**.

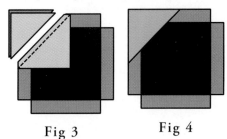

Fig 3   Fig 4

5. Repeat steps 2–5 for remaining three corners to complete pillow top, **Fig 5**.

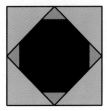

Fig 5

6. Refer to Basic Pillow, page 12, to complete pillow.

Japanese Fish

Pillow size: 16" square
Technique: Stitch & Flip, page 6

Materials
Fat quarter, orange
½ yd Japanese fish print (includes backing)
16" pillow form

Cutting
4 – 6½" x 4½" rectangles, Japanese fish print
4 – 2½" x 4½" rectangles, Japanese fish print
24 – 2½" squares, Japanese fish print
4 – 6½" x 4½" rectangles, orange
4 – 2½" x 4½" rectangles, orange
1 – 16½" square, Japanese fish print (backing)

Instructions
1. Since the fish print fabric is directional, special consideration must be given when piecing so that fabric will be facing the right direction. With the top edge of the square at the top, draw a diagonal

line from top left corner to bottom right corner on the wrong side of 12 of the 2½" squares (A), **Fig 6**. Repeat for remaining 12 squares (B), except start from the upper right corner to lower left corner, **Fig 7**.

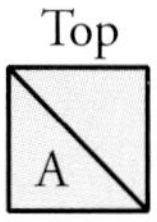

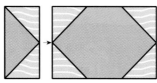

Fig 6

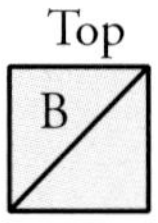

Fig 7

2. Place 2½" A square right sides together with upper left corner of orange 4½" x 6½" rectangle. Be sure to turn the square so that the top edge is facing right and diagonal line is going from top right to bottom left; sew along drawn line, **Fig 8**.

3. Trim ¼" from sewing line and flip triangle over, **Fig 9**.

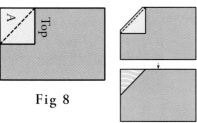

Fig 8

Fig 9

4. Repeat at remaining corners, being sure that 2½" print square is rotated in correct direction, **Fig 10**.

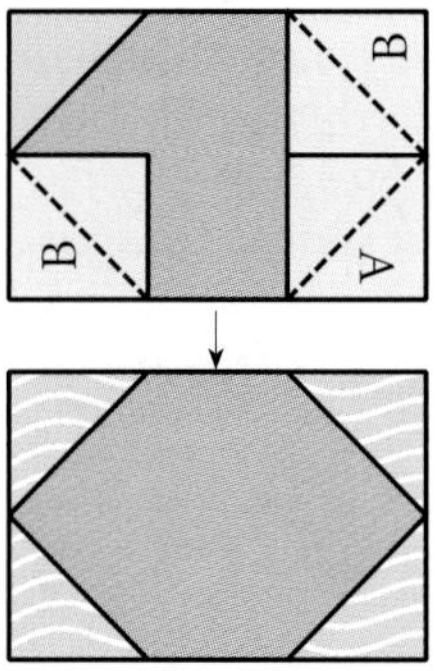

5. Repeat stitch and flip method for 2½" x 4½" orange rectangles and remaining fish print squares, **Fig 11**. Again, note positions of fish print squares.

Fig 10

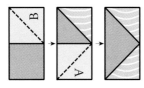

Fig 11

6. Sew units from step 4 and step 5 together to complete Fish block, **Fig 12**. Repeat for three more Fish blocks.

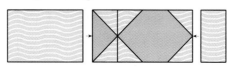

Fig 12

7. For rows 1 and 3, sew 4½" x 6½" fish print rectangle, Fish block and 2½" x 4½" fish print rectangle together, **Fig 13**.

Fig 13

8. For rows 2 and 4, sew 2½" x 4½" fish print rectangle, Fish block and 4½" x 6½" fish print rectangle together, **Fig 14**.

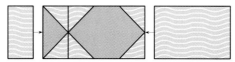

Fig 14

9. Sew rows together to complete pillow top, **Fig 15**.

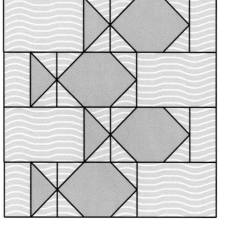

Fig 15

10. Refer to Basic Pillow, page 12, to complete pillow.

Chinese Block

Pillow Size: 12" square plus 2" flange
Technique: Stitch & Flip, page 6; Half-Square Triangles, page 5

Materials
½ yd Oriental print (includes backing)
Fat quarter, tan print
Fat quarter, black
12" pillow form

Cutting
1 – 8½" square, Oriental print
4 – 2½" squares, tan print
4 – 3" squares, tan print
4 – 3" squares, black
4 – 2½" x 4½" rectangles, black
4 – 4½" squares, black
2 – 2½" x 12½" strips, Oriental print (flange)
2 – 2½" x 16½" strips, Oriental print (flange)
1 – 16½" square, Oriental print (backing)

Instructions

1. Use the stitch and flip method to sew 4½" black squares to 8½" Oriental print square, **Fig 16**.

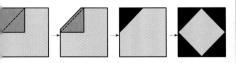

Fig 16

2. Draw diagonal line on wrong side of 3" tan print squares.

3. Place 3" tan print square right sides together with 3" black square. Sew ¼" from each side of diagonal line, **Fig 17**.

Fig 17

4. Cut along drawn line for two triangle/squares, **Fig 18**. Repeat with remaining tan print and black 3" squares.

Fig 18

5. Sew a triangle/square to each side of a 2½" x 4½" black rectangle noting position, **Fig 19**. Repeat three more times.

Fig 19

6. Sew unit from step 5 to opposite sides of unit from step 1, **Fig 20**.

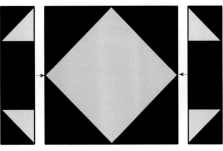

Fig 20

7. Sew tan print square to remaining units from step 5 and sew to top and bottom edge to complete pillow top, **Fig 21**.

Fig 21

8. Sew 2½" x 12½" oriental print strips to sides of pillow top; press. Sew 2½" x 16½" oriental print strips to top and bottom to complete pillow top.

9. Refer to Pillows With a Flange, page 13, to complete pillow.

Oriental Fan

Pillow Size: 14"
Technique: Curved Piecing, page 6

Materials

½ yd lt background (includes backing)
10" squares, blue print, yellow print, black print
14" pillow form
2 yds tassel fringe

Cutting

Note: *Cut out Fan shapes using patterns on page 85. Trace pattern onto fabric; add ¼" all around when cutting out.*

1 – Fan Blade A each, yellow and blue
1 – Fan Blade B each, yellow and blue
1 – Fan Handle C, black print
2 – 4½" squares, lt background

Instructions

1. Sew Fan Blades A and B together, alternating colors, **Fig 22**. Press seams to one side.

Fig 22

2. Place Fan Blades and Fan Handle right sides together, matching center points; pin in place, **Fig 23**. Place pin at each end, **Fig 24**.

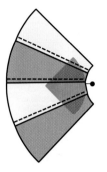 

Fig 24

Fig 23

3. With Fan Blade section on top, sew slowly along curved edge bringing raw edges even as you sew. Press seam toward Fan Handle.

4. Press outer curved edge of fan under ¼". Place on background square and pin in place. Sew curved edge in place using a machine zigzag and invisible or matching thread, **Fig 25**. *Hint: Baste straight edges of fan to background fabric if desired.*

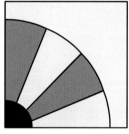

Fig 25

5. Refer to Pillows With Trimmed Edges, page 12, to finish pillow.

Chinese Puzzle

Pillow Size: 14" square
Technique: Half-Square Triangles, page 5

Materials

Fat quarters, white, pink print, blue print
½ yd backing
14" pillow form
2 yds beaded cording

Cutting

8 – 4½" squares, white
5 – 4½" squares, pink print
5 – 4½" squares, blue print
1 – 14½" square, backing

Instructions

1. Draw diagonal line on wrong side of all white squares.

2. Place white square and blue print square right sides together. Sew ¼" from each side of drawn line, **Fig 26**.

Fig 26

3. Cut along drawn line and press open for two triangle/squares, **Fig 27**. Repeat for three more triangle/squares.

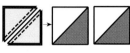

Fig 27

4. Repeat steps 2 and 3 with white and pink print squares, **Fig 28**.

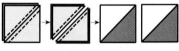

Fig 28

5. Draw diagonal line on wrong side of remaining pink print square; place right sides together with blue print square and sew ¼" from each side of drawn line. Cut along drawn line and press open, **Fig 29**. Trim squares to 4" square.

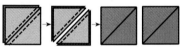

Fig 29

6. Place triangle/squares according to **Fig 30**. Sew triangle/squares together in rows; press seams for rows in opposite directions. Sew rows together to complete pillow top.

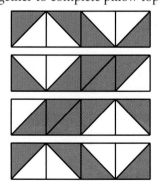

Fig 30

7. Refer to Pillows With Trimmed Edges, page 12, to finish pillow.

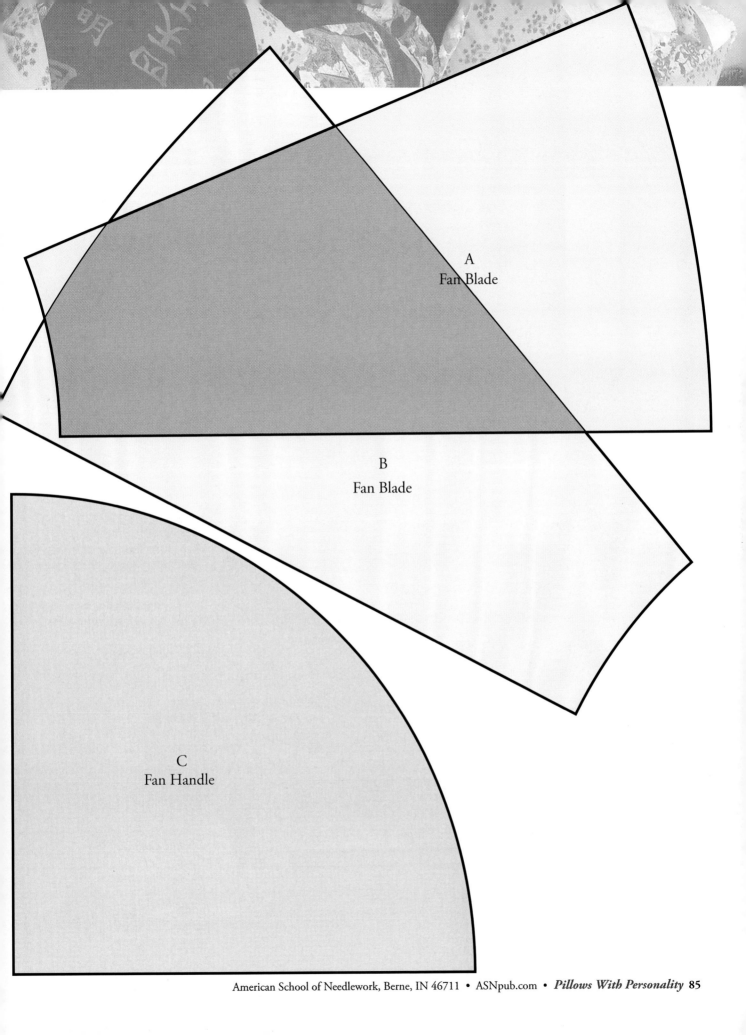

A
Fan Blade

B
Fan Blade

C
Fan Handle

For Her Highness

Surround your favorite little girl with these pillows to remind her that she will always be your little princess.
There are foundation-pieced castle and frog blocks as well as easy-appliqué and pieced crown blocks.
Combine four pieced Four Crown blocks to make a king-size pillow.

Frog or Prince? Pillow

Pillow size: 14" square
Technique: Foundation Piecing, page 8

Materials
Fat quarters, lt green, dk green, yellow
Scraps, white, black
¼ yd background print
½ yd blue print (border and backing)
12" pillow form
2 yds ruffle trim

Cutting
Note: *Foundation piecing does not require cutting exact pieces.*

2 – 1½" x 8½" strips, yellow (first border)
2 – 1½" x 10½" strips, yellow (first border)
2 – 2½" x 10½" strips, blue print (second border)
2 – 2½" x 14½" strips, blue print (second border)
1 – 14½" square background (backing)

Instructions

1. Make Frog block using pattern on page 88 and referring to Foundation Piecing, **Fig 1**.

Fig 1

2. Add first border to the sides, then to the top and bottom; add second border in same manner, **Fig 2**.

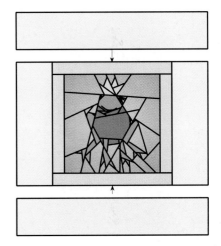

Fig 2

3. Remove paper foundation.

4. Refer to Pillows With Trimmed Edges, page 12, to finish pillow.

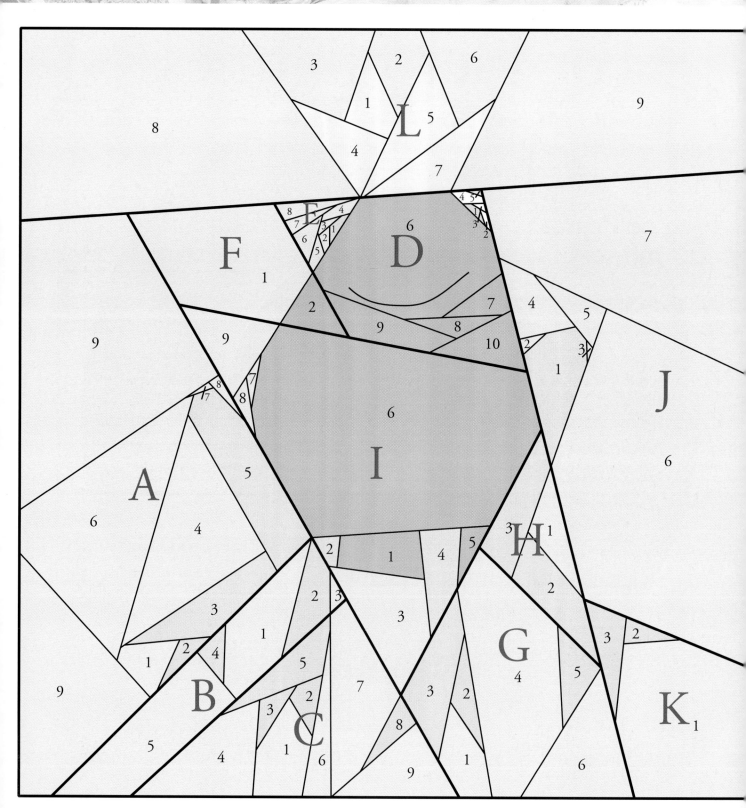

Frog Foundation Pattern

Castle

Pillow Size: 12" plus 2"-wide flange
Technique: Foundation Piecing, page 8

Materials

Fat quarters, lt pink, pink print, lt blue
Scraps, green, lavender, dk pink
½ yd castle print (border and backing)
12" pillow form

Cutting

Note: *Foundation piecing does not require cutting exact pieces.*

2 – 3½" x 10½" strips, castle print (flange)
2 – 3½" x 16½" strips, castle print (flange)
1 – 16½" square, castle print (backing)

Instructions

1. Make Castle block using patterns on pages 89 and 90 and referring to Foundation Piecing, **Fig 3**.

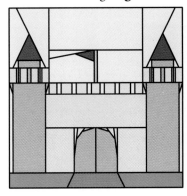

Fig 3

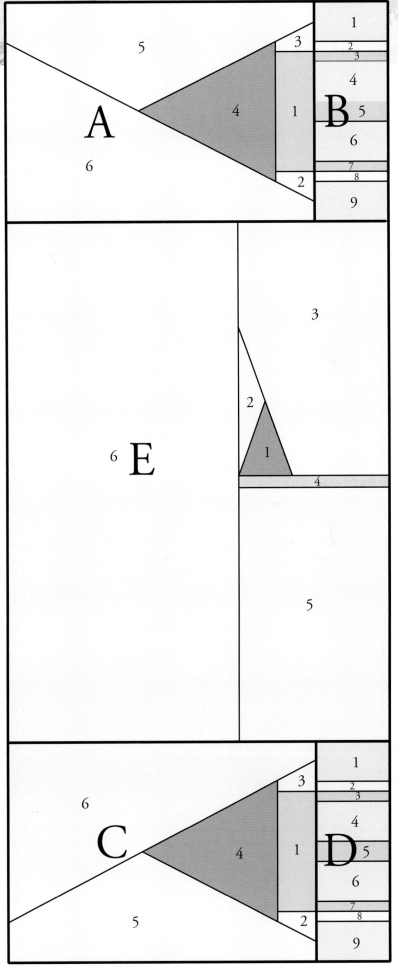

Castle Foundation Pattern

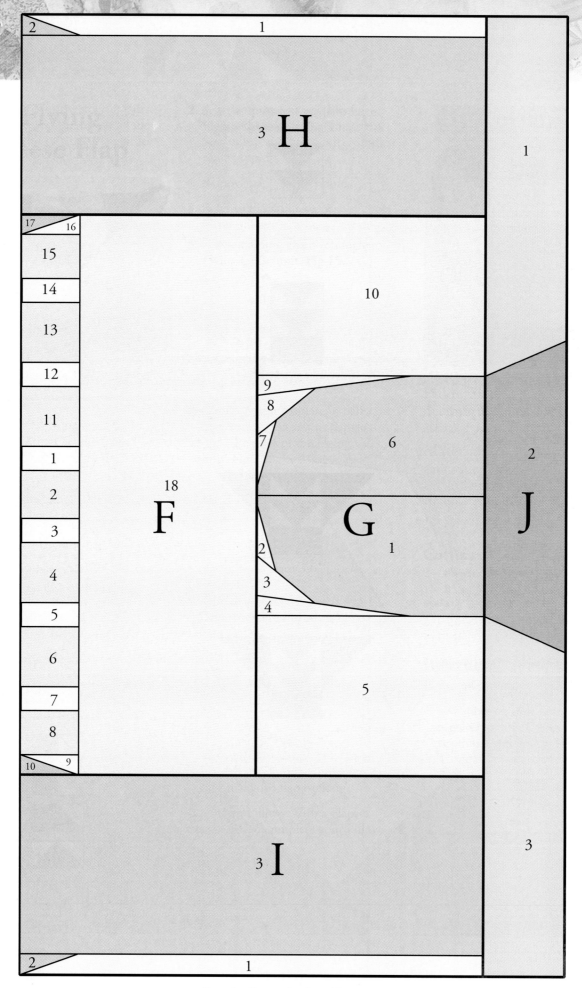

Castle Foundation Pattern

2. Sew a 3½" x 10½" castle print strip to each side of Castle block. Press seams toward border. Sew a 3½" x 16½" strip to top and bottom, **Fig 4**. Press seams toward border.

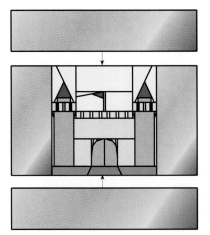

Fig 4

3. Remove paper foundation.

4. Refer to Pillows With a Flange, page 13, to finish pillow. *Note: After sewing on border, draw a line 1" from seam using a removable fabric pen or pencil. This will be the sewing line for the flange,* **Fig 5**.

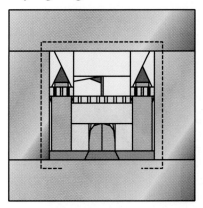

Fig 5

Princess

Pillow Size: 14" square
Technique: Easy Machine Appliqué, page 7

Materials

Fat quarter, yellow
Scrap, purple
½ yd pink print
1 yd fine pink tulle
14" pillow form
Large button, charm, etc.

Cutting

Note: *Refer to Easy Machine Appliqué, for cutting instructions.*

2 – 14½" squares, pink print
2 – 30" squares, pink tulle

Instructions

1. Make pillow top using pattern on page 92 and referring to Easy Machine Appliqué, **Fig 6**.

Fig 6

2. Place tulle squares together; sew two rows of gathering stitches on three sides of both layers of pink tulle, **Fig 7**. Begin and end on each side, sewing rows about ⅛" and ¼" from edge.

Fig 7

3. Pull stitches to gather tulle to 14½" on the three sides.

4. Place tulle on right side of pillow top with non-gathered edge at bottom, **Fig 8**. Pin then baste the three gathered sides in place.

Fig 8

5. Refer to Basic Pillow, page 12, to finish pillow. Be sure not to catch non-gathered edge in stitching.

6. After pillow is finished, bring non-gathered tulle edge to top middle, **Fig 9**; tack in place. Add decorative button, charm, etc., to finish.

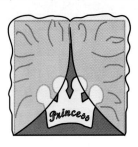

Fig 9

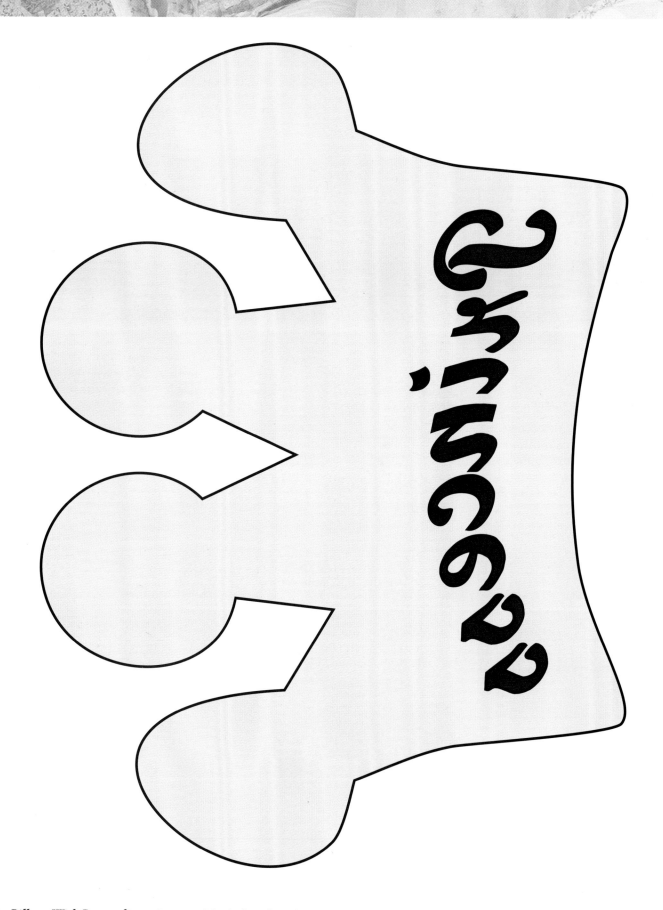

Four Crowns

Pillow Size: 16" square
Technique: Half-Square Triangles,
   page 5

Materials
Fat quarters, dk pink, lt pink, purple,
   lt background
½ yd pink print, border (includes
   backing)
16" pillow form
2 yds ruffle

Cutting
2 – 2½" squares, dk pink (A)
2 – 3" squares, dk pink (D)
1 – 5" square, dk pink (H)
2 – 2½" squares, lt pink (B)
2 – 3" squares, lt pink (E)
1 – 5" square, lt pink (I)
1 – 4½" square, purple (G)
8 – 2½" squares, lt background (C)
4 – 3" squares, lt background (F)
2 – 3⅝" squares, lt background (J)
2 – 2½" x 12½" strips, pink print
2 – 2½" x 16½" strips, pink print
1 – 16½" square, pink print (backing)

Instructions

1. Cut J squares in half diagonally. Sew
a triangle to each side of G square,
Fig 10.

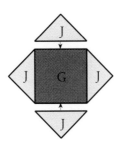

Fig 10

2. Cut H and I squares in half
diagonally. Sew H triangles to
opposite sides of G/J unit; sew I
triangles to remaining sides, **Fig 11**.

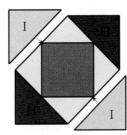

Fig 11

3. Mark diagonal line on wrong side of
each F square. Place F square right
sides together with D square; sew
¼" from each side of diagonal line,
Fig 12. Repeat.

Fig 12

4. Cut along diagonal line for a total of
four triangle/squares, **Fig 13**.

Fig 13

5. Repeat steps 3 and 4 with F and E
squares, **Fig 14**.

Fig 14

6. Sew E/F triangle/square to C square;
repeat three more times referring to
Fig 15 for positions.

Fig 15

7. Repeat step 6 with D/F triangle/
squares, **Fig 16**.

Fig 16

8. Sew C/D/F unit to C/E/F unit;
repeat three more times referring
to **Fig 17** for positions.

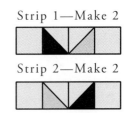

Fig 17

9. Sew strip 1 units to sides of block noting placement, **Fig 18**.

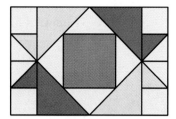

Fig 18

10. Sew an A square to one end of strip 2; sew B square to other end, **Fig 19**. Repeat for other strip 2.

Make 2

Fig 19

11. Sew to top and bottom to complete block, **Fig 20**.

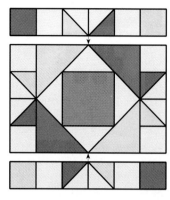

Fig 20

12. Sew 2½" x 12½" pink print strips to sides of block; press seam toward border. Sew 2½" x 16½" pink print strips to top and bottom of block, **Fig 21**; press seam toward border.

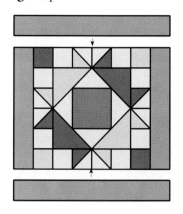

Fig 21

13. Refer to Pillows With Trimmed Edges, page 12, for ready-made ruffle or Pillows With Ruffles, page 14, to finish pillow.

King-Size

Pillow Size: 30" square
Technique: Half-Square Triangles, page 5

Materials
¾ yd white
Fat quarters, purple, lt yellow, dk yellow
1 yd yellow/blue print (border and backing)
⅜ yd purple print
30" pillow form

Cutting
8 – 2½" squares, dk yellow (A)
4 – 4½" squares, purple (G)
8 – 2½" squares, lt yellow (B)
32 – 2½" squares, white (C)
16 – 3" squares, white (F)
8 – 3⅝" squares, white (J)
4 – 5" squares, dk yellow (H)
8 – 3" squares, dk yellow (D)
8 – 3" squares, lt yellow (E)
4 – 5" squares, lt yellow (I)
2 – 2½" x 12½" strips, purple print
1 – 2½" x 26½" strip, purple print
2 – 2½" x 26½" strips, yellow/blue print
2 – 2½" x 30½" strips, yellow/blue print

Instructions

1. Make four Four Crowns blocks referring to instructions on previous page and substituting the colors above, **Fig 22**.

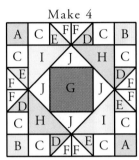

Make 4

Fig 22

2. Sew blocks in pairs with 2½" x 12½" purple print strips in between, **Fig 23**.

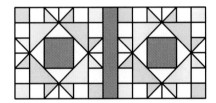

Fig 23

3. Sew pairs of blocks together with a 2½" x 26½" purple print strip in between; sew a 2½" x 26½" yellow/blue print strip to sides, **Fig 24**.

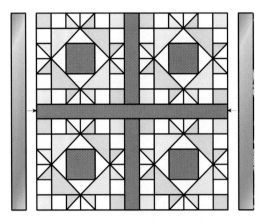

Fig 24

4. Sew 2½" x 30½" yellow/blue print strips to top and bottom to complete pillow top, **Fig 25**.

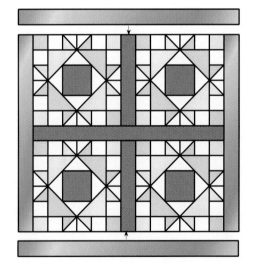

Fig 25

5. Refer to Basic Pillow, page 12, to complete your pillow.

Raining Cats & Dogs

If you love dogs and cats, you'll love this ensemble of pillows. Included is a houseful of playful pups and cool cats, a Nine-Patch with a hidden surprise, a couple of "framed" critters and, finally, a pillow with cats and dogs going round and round.

Houseful of Pets

Pillow Size: 14" square
Technique: Stitch & Flip, page 6

Materials
½ yd animal print (includes backing)
Fat quarters, red, green, blue
14" pillow form
2 yds large rickrack

Cutting
2 – 5¾" x 7½" rectangles, animal print
1 – 1½" x 7½" strip, red
2 – 2¾" squares, red
1 – 2¾" x 12" strip, red
2 – 1¾" x 9¾" strips, red
1 – 5¼" x 14½" strip, green
2 – 5¼" squares, blue
1 – 14½" square, backing

Instructions

1. Using the stitch and flip method, sew a 2¾" red square to the upper left corner of an animal print rectangle, **Fig 1**. Repeat with another square and rectangle, except place red square in upper right corner, **Fig 2**.

Fig 1

Fig 2

2. Sew the animal print rectangles together with 1½" x 7½" red strip in between, **Fig 3**.

Fig 3

3. Sew 2¾" x 12" red strip to top edge of animal print rectangles, **Fig 4**.

Fig 4

4. Sew a 1¾" x 9¾" red strip to each side of animal print section, **Fig 5**.

Fig 5

5. Sew green rectangle to top edge of animal print section, **Fig 6**.

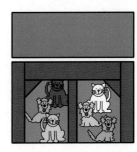

Fig 6

6. Using the stitch and flip method, sew a blue square to each side of green rectangle to complete pillow top, **Fig 7**.

Fig 7

7. Refer to Pillows With Trimmed Edges, page 12, to finish pillow with rickrack along outer edges.

Where's the Kitty?

Pillow Size: 14" square
Technique: Easy Machine Appliqué, page 7

Materials

Fat quarters yellow, red
½ yd blue (includes backing)
Fat quarter, animal print*
14" pillow form
*Depending on the size and spacing of the individual animal motifs, you may need more than one fat quarter for five separate animal motifs.

Cutting

Note: *Refer to Easy Machine Appliqué to cut out five animal motifs. Photographed model uses four dogs and one cat.*

4 – 5" squares, yellow (corners)
1 – 5½" x 5½" square, yellow (center)
4 – 5½" x 5" rectangles, blue
1 – 15¼" square, red (flap)

Instructions

1. Fuse an animal motif to each blue rectangle, **Fig 8**. ***Hint:*** *Fuse a dog to three of the rectangles and a cat on the remaining rectangle. The cat can then "hide" from the dogs.*

Fig 8

2. For rows 1 and 3 of the Nine-Patch, sew a 5" yellow square on each side of a blue rectangle, **Fig 9**.

Fig 9

3. For row 2, sew a blue rectangle to each side of a 5½" yellow square, **Fig 10**.

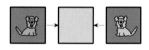

Fig 10

4. Sew rows 1, 2 and 3 together to form Nine Patch, **Fig 11**.

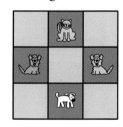

Fig 11

5. Cut red square into quarters, **Fig 12**. (You will have two left over.)

Fig 12

6. For flap, place red triangles right sides together; sew along both short sides, **Fig 13**.

Fig 13

7. Turn triangles right sides out; press. Fuse an animal motif on top triangle, **Fig 14**.

Fig 14

8. Refer to Pillows With a Flap, page 13, to finish pillow.

Animals in the Middle

Pillow Size: 16" square
Technique: Rotary Cutting, page 4

Materials

½ yd animal print (includes backing)
Fat quarters, yellow, green
16" pillow form
2 yds cording

Cutting

4 – 4½" squares, yellow
4 – 4½" x 8½" rectangles, green
1 – 8½" square, animal print
1 – 16½" square, animal print (backing)

Instructions

1. For rows 1 and 3, sew a yellow square to each end of a green rectangle, **Fig 15**.

Fig 15

2. For row 2, sew green rectangle to opposite sides of animal print square, **Fig 16**.

Fig 16

3. Sew rows 1, 2 and 3 together to complete pillow top, **Fig 17**.

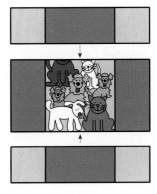

Fig 17

4. Refer to Pillows With Trimmed Edges, page 12, to finish pillow.

Fenced In

Pillow Size: 16" square
Technique: Half-Square Triangles,
   page 5

Materials
½ yd animal print (includes backing)
Fat quarters, red, blue
16" pillow form

Cutting
4 – 2½" x 8½" strips, red
4 – 2½" x 8½" strips, blue
2 – 5" squares, red
2 – 5" squares, blue
1 – 8½" square, animal print
1 – 16½" squares, animal print
   (backing)

Instructions

1. Sew a 2½" x 8½" red and blue strip together lengthwise, **Fig 18**. Repeat three more times.

Fig 18

2. Draw diagonal line on wrong side of blue squares. Place red and blue square right sides together; sew ¼" from each side of drawn line. Cut along drawn line to get two triangle/squares, **Fig 19**. Repeat with remaining squares.

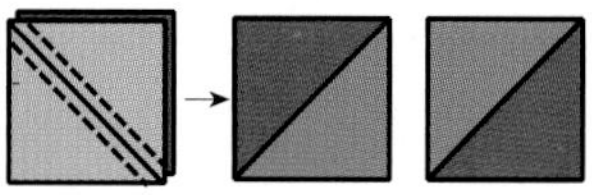

Fig 19

3. For rows 1 and 3, sew triangle/square to each side of red/blue strips, noting placement, **Fig 20**.

Fig 20

4. For row 2, sew red/blue strips to opposite sides of animal print square; be sure red strip is next to animal print, **Fig 21**.

Fig 21

5. Sew rows 1, 2 and 3 together to complete pillow top, **Fig 22**.

Fig 22

6. Refer to Basic Pillow, page 12, to finish pillow.

Cats & Dogs on a Roll

Pillow Size: 14" x 5" neck roll
Technique: Easy Machine Appliqué,
  page 7

Materials
Fat quarters, blue, yellow, red
¼–½ yd animal print
1 yd each blue and yellow cording
14" x 5" neck-roll pillow form

Cutting
Note: Refer to Easy Machine Appliqué to cut out several assorted animal motifs.

1 – 14½" x 19½" rectangle each, blue, yellow, red

Instructions

1. Fuse animal motifs in pleasing arrangement onto one 14½" x 19½" blue rectangle, **Fig 23**.

Fig 23

2. Sew red and yellow 14½" x 19½" rectangles to sides of 14½" x 19½" rectangle to complete pillow top, **Fig 24**.

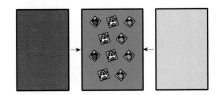

Fig 24

3. Fold pillow top in half crosswise with right sides together; sew across edge opposite fold, **Fig 25**. Press seam open.

Fig 25

4. Fold raw edge of short side over ¼"; fold again until folded end covers seam allowance and stitch along first fold, **Fig 26**. Turn pillow top right side out.

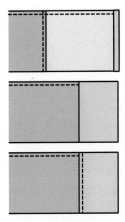

Fig 26

5. Place pillow form inside pillow top. Tie each end with cording to finish pillow. ***Note:*** *Knot ends of cording to keep from raveling.*

It's a Guy Thing!

This group of five pillows with outdoor-themed fabric and masculine-themed blocks will be a perfect addition for the den, game room or your favorite guy.

Bachelor's Puzzle

Pillow Size: 14" square plus 2"-wide flange
Technique: Half-Square Triangles, page 5

Materials
Fat quarters, beige, lt blue, dk blue
⅝ yd theme print (includes backing)
14" pillow form

Cutting
4 – 4" squares, beige
4 – 4½" squares, beige
4 – 4½" squares, lt blue
4 – 4½" squares, dk blue
2 – 2½" x 14½" strips, theme print*
   (flange)
2 – 2½" x 18½" strips, theme print*
   (flange)
1 – 18½" square, backing fabric
*If theme print is directional, be sure
   to cut the side strips first on the
   lengthwise grain and the top and
   bottom strips crosswise. You may need
   to purchase more fabric.

Instructions

1. Cut all 4½" squares in half diagonally.

2. Make four of each triangle/square combination, **Fig 1**. Trim squares to 4" square.

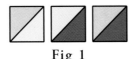

Fig 1

3. Place squares and triangle/squares according to **Fig 2.** Sew squares together in rows; press seams for rows in alternating directions. Sew rows together.

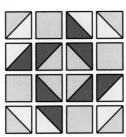

Fig 2

4. Sew 2½" x 14½" theme print strips to sides of block; sew 2½" x 18½" theme print strips to top and bottom.

5. Refer to Pillows With a Flange, page 13, to finish pillow.

Card Tricks

Pillow Size: 12" square plus 2"-wide flange
Technique: Half-Square Triangles, page 5

Materials
Fat quarters, blue, gold, green, brown
Fat quarter, beige
Fat quarter, theme print
Fat quarter, backing
12" pillow form

Cutting
1 – 5" square, blue, gold, green, brown
2 – 5" squares, beige
1 – 5¼" square, blue, gold, green,
   brown and beige
*2 – 2½" x 12½" strips, theme print
   (flange)
*2 – 2½" x 16½" strips, theme print
   (flange)
1 – 16½" square, backing
*If theme print is directional, be sure
   to cut the side strips first on the
   lengthwise grain and the top and
   bottom strips crosswise.

Instructions

1. Cut all 5" squares in half diagonally.

2. Sew a beige triangle to one triangle of each remaining color, **Fig 3**. Press seam toward dark fabric. Trim squares to 4½" square.

Fig 3

3. Cut all 5¼" squares diagonally in quarters, **Fig 4**. Sew a beige triangle to a triangle of each of the remaining colors, **Fig 5**. Press seam toward dark fabrics. Sew to large triangles as shown in **Fig 6**.

Fig 4

Fig 5

Fig 6

4. For center triangle, sew a gold triangle to a blue triangle, noting positions, **Fig 7**; press seam toward blue.

Fig 7

5. Sew a green triangle to a brown triangle, noting positions, **Fig 8**; press seam toward green.

Fig 8

6. Sew triangles from steps 5 and 6 together, **Fig 9**.

Fig 9

7. Trim all squares to 4½" square.

8. Place squares according to **Fig 10**, noting positions. Sew squares together in rows; press seams for rows in alternating directions. Sew rows together.

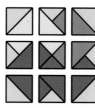

Fig 10

9. Sew 2½" x 12½" theme print strips to sides first, then sew 2½" x 16½" theme print strips to top and bottom. Press seams toward theme print.

10. Refer to Pillows With a Flange, page 13, to finish pillow.

Round Star

Pillow Size: 14" round
Technique: Foundation Piecing, page 8

Materials

Fat quarters, dk blue, dk green, beige
Fat quarter, backing
2 yds cording

Cutting

Note: Foundation piecing does not require cutting exact pieces. Use pattern on page 73 to make circle for backing.

1 – 14½" Circle, backing

Instructions

1. Refer to Foundation Piecing to make four sections using pattern on page 105. Trim outer edge ¼" from straight edges and ¼" from curved edge, **Fig 11**.

Fig 11

2. Sew sections together in pairs, then sew pairs together, **Fig 12**.

3. Stay-stitch around edge of pillow front then remove paper foundation.

4. Refer to Pillows With Trimmed Edges, page 12, to finish pillow.

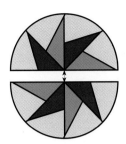

Fig 12

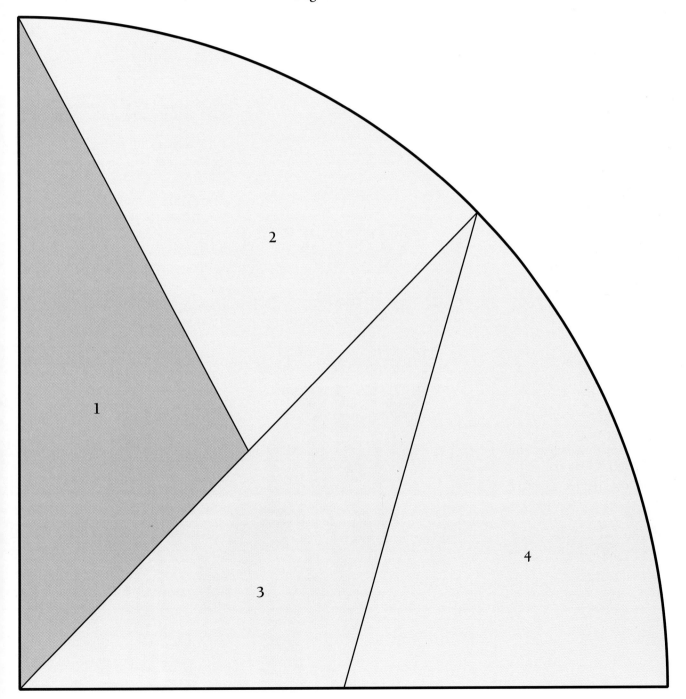

Round Star Foundation Pattern

Flying Geese Flap

Pillow Size: 12" square
Technique: Stitch & Flip, page 6

Materials
½ yd beige print
Fat quarter, blue
10" squares, beige, green
12" pillow form

Cutting
1 – 5" square, blue
1 – 9½" square, blue (flap backing)
3 – 2½" x 4½" rectangles, green
4 – 2½" squares, beige
2 – 12½" squares, beige print

Instructions
1. Sew two beige squares to a green rectangle using the stitch and flip method, **Fig 13**. Repeat.

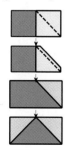

Fig 13

2. Sew the units just made to form Flying Geese unit, **Fig 14**.

Fig 14

3. Sew remaining green rectangle to Flying Geese unit, **Fig 15**.

Fig 15

4. Cut the 5" blue square in half diagonally, then sew a triangle to opposite sides of the Flying Geese unit, **Fig 16**.

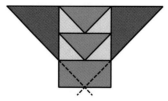

Fig 16

5. Trim diagonal edges even, **Fig 17**. Stay-stitch around edges of triangle.

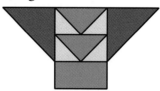

Fig 17

6. Cut 9½" blue square in half diagonally for flap backing.

7. Refer to Pillows With a Flap, page 13, to complete your pillow.

Birds in the Air

Pillow Size: 14" square
Technique: Half-Square Triangles, page 5

Materials
Fat quarters, lt gold, med gold
Fat quarter, dk blue
Fat quarter, backing
14" pillow form
2 yds cording

Cutting
2 – 8" squares, med gold
1 – 8" square, dk blue
5 – 4½" squares, dk blue
2 – 4½" squares, lt gold
1 – 14½" square, backing fabric

Instructions
1. Cut all squares in half diagonally.

2. Sew small dk blue triangle to small lt gold triangle, **Fig 18**. Repeat two more times. Trim squares to 4" square.

Fig 18

3. Sew small dk blue triangles to small lt gold edges of triangle/squares just made, **Fig 19**. Trim diagonal edge so pieced triangle is same size as med gold triangle.

Fig 19

4. Sew units from step 3 to large med gold triangles, **Fig 20**. Trim squares to 7½" square.

Fig 20

5. Sew remaining large med gold triangle to large dk blue triangle, **Fig 21**. Trim square to 7½" square.

Fig 21

6. Place squares according to **Fig 22**. Sew together in rows; press seams for rows in opposite directions. Sew rows together to complete pillow top.

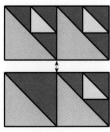

Fig 22

7. Refer to Pillows With Trimmed Edges, page 12, to complete your pillow.

Combo Floor

Pillow Size: 30" square
Technique: Half-Square Triangles, page 5

Materials
½ yd beige
⅜ yd rust
10" square, med gold
⅝ yd dk green
¼ yd lt green
¼ yd med green
1 yd backing

Cutting
16 – 4" squares, beige
4 – 4½" squares, rust
2 – 4½" squares, med gold
16 – 4½" squares, dk green
8 – 4½" squares, lt green
12 – 4½" squares, med green
6 – 4½" squares, beige
2 – 2½" x 14½" strips, rust (sashing)
1 – 2½" x 30½" strip, rust (sashing)
1 – 30½" x 30½" square, backing fabric

Instructions
1. Make triangle/squares in the combinations shown in **Fig 23**. Trim to 4" square.

Make 16 Make 12 Make 12

Make 4   Make 4

Fig 23

2. Make four Bachelor Puzzle blocks referring to instructions on page 103, **Fig 24**.

Make 4

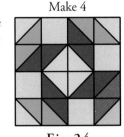

Fig 24

3. Sew two blocks together with 2½" x 14½" rust strips in between, **Fig 25**; repeat. Note position of blocks.

Fig 25

4. Sew pairs of blocks together with 2½" x 30½" rust sashing strip in between, **Fig 26**.

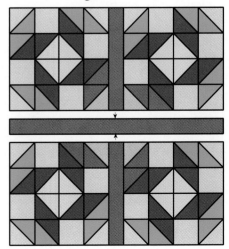

Fig 26

5. Refer to Basic Pillow, page 12, to complete pillow.

Pocketful of Posies

This group of pillows will add a soft floral accent to any living room, bedroom or den. They come in a variety of sizes and shapes—from a patchwork neck-roll pillow to a round appliqué as well as a square foundation-pieced pillow.

Nine-Patch Posies

Pillow Size: 12" square plus 2"-wide flange
Technique: Half-Square Triangles, page 5

Materials
Fat quarter, floral print
½ yd burgundy (includes flange and backing)
12" pillow form

Cutting
4 – 4½" squares, floral print
4 – 2½" squares, floral print
4 – 3" squares, floral print
1 – 4½" square, burgundy
4 – 2½" squares, burgundy
4 – 3" squares, burgundy
2 – 2½" x 12½" strips, burgundy (flange)
2 – 2½" x 16½" strips, burgundy (flange)
1 – 16½" square, burgundy (backing)

Instructions

1. Draw diagonal line on wrong side of 3" floral print squares. Place 3" floral print and burgundy squares right sides together; sew ¼" from each side of drawn line, **Fig 1**.

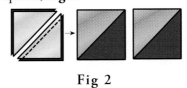

Fig 1

2. Cut along drawn line for two triangle squares, **Fig 2**.

Fig 2

3. Repeat steps 1 and 2 for remaining 3" squares.

4. Trim triangle/squares to 2½".

5. Sew triangle/square to 2½" floral square noting placement, **Fig 3**. Repeat three more times.

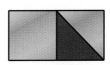

Fig 3

6. Sew triangle/square to 2½" burgundy square noting placement, **Fig 4**. Repeat three more times.

Fig 4

7. Sew pairs of squares from steps 5 and 6 to complete four pieced squares, **Fig 5**.

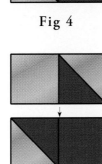

Fig 5

8. For rows 1 and 3 of Nine-Patch, sew a pieced square on opposite sides of 4½" floral square noting placement, **Fig 6**. Repeat.

Rows 1 & 3

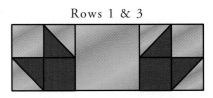

Fig 6

9. For row 2 of Nine Patch, sew 4½" floral square to opposite sides of a 4½" burgundy square, **Fig 7**.

Row 2

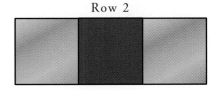

Fig 7

10. Sew rows together to complete Nine Patch, **Fig 8**.

Fig 8

11. Sew 2½" x 12½" burgundy strips to sides of Nine-Patch, then sew 2½" x 16½" burgundy strips to top and bottom, **Fig 9**.

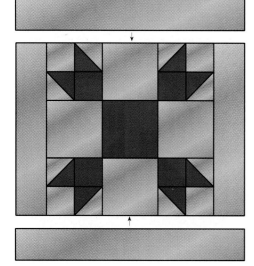

Fig 9

12. Refer to Pillows With a Flange, page 13, to finish pillow.

Posy Vine

Pillow Size: 14" square plus 2"-wide flange
Technique: Easy Machine Appliqué, page 7

Materials
Fat quarters, pink, dk green
Scrap, gold
⅝ yd dk green (includes flange and backing)
Fat quarter, lt green (background)
½ yd paper-backed fusible web
14" pillow form

Cutting
Note: Refer to Easy Machine Applique to cut out patterns found here and on page 113.

5 – Flower, pink,
5 – Flower Center, gold
4 – Leaf, dk green
1 – ¼" x 20" bias strip with paper-backed fusible web, dk green (stem)
1 – 14½" square, lt green (background)
2 – 2½" x 14½" strips, dk green (flange)
2 – 2½" x 18½" strips, dk green (flange)
1 – 18½" square, dk green (backing)

Instructions

1. Following manufacturer's directions, fuse stem, Flowers and Leaves to lt green background square referring to **Fig 10**. *Note: Bias strip with fusible web will curve into gentle curves. Machine-zigzag with invisible thread around each shape if desired.*

Fig 10

2. Sew 2½" x 14½" dk green strips to sides of appliqué; sew 2½" x 18½" dk green strips to top and bottom, **Fig 11**.

Fig 11

3. Refer to Pillows With a Flange, page 13, to finish pillow.

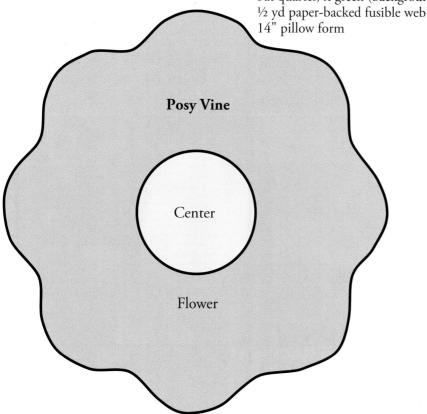

Posy Vine

Center

Flower

Pretty Posy

Pillow Size: 14" square
Technique: Foundation Piecing, page 8

Materials

Fat quarters, lt pink, green
Scraps, gold, med pink, burgundy
Fat quarter, backing
2 yds scalloped fringe trim
14" pillow form

Cutting

Note: *Foundation piecing does not require cutting of exact pieces.*

14½" square, backing fabric

Instructions

1. Make four Pretty Posy blocks using the pattern on page 112. Sew blocks together in pairs then sew pairs together, **Fig 12**.

2. Remove paper foundation.

3. Refer to Pillows With Trimmed Edges, page 12, to finish pillow.

Fig 12

Rosy Posy

Pillow Size: 14" round
Technique: Easy Machine Appliqué, page 7

Materials

Fat quarters, lt pink, med pink, dk pink, gold
½ yd green (includes backing)
2 yds looped cord trim

Cutting

Note: *Use pattern on page 71 for 14½" circles.*

3 – Petal, lt pink
3 – Petal, med pink
18 – Petal dk pink
2 – Flower Center, gold
2 – 14½" Circle, green

Instructions

1. Place a light pink Petal right sides together with a dark pink Petal; sew along entire outer edge, **Fig 13**. Repeat for remaining lt pink, med pink and dk pink Petals.

Fig 13

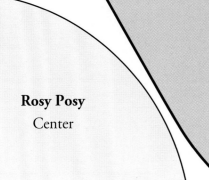

Rosy Posy

Center

Rosy Posy

Loose petals

Petal
Make six dark
and six light

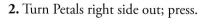

2. Turn Petals right side out; press.

3. Arrange petals on 14½" green circle being sure they are about 1" from outer edge, **Fig 14**. Pin Petals in place.

Fig 14

4. Place gold Flower Centers right sides together; sew along entire outer edge, **Fig 15**.

Fig 15

5. Pull Flower Center circles apart and carefully cut a small slit in center of one of the circles, **Fig 16**.

6. Turn right side out through slit; press.

Fig 16

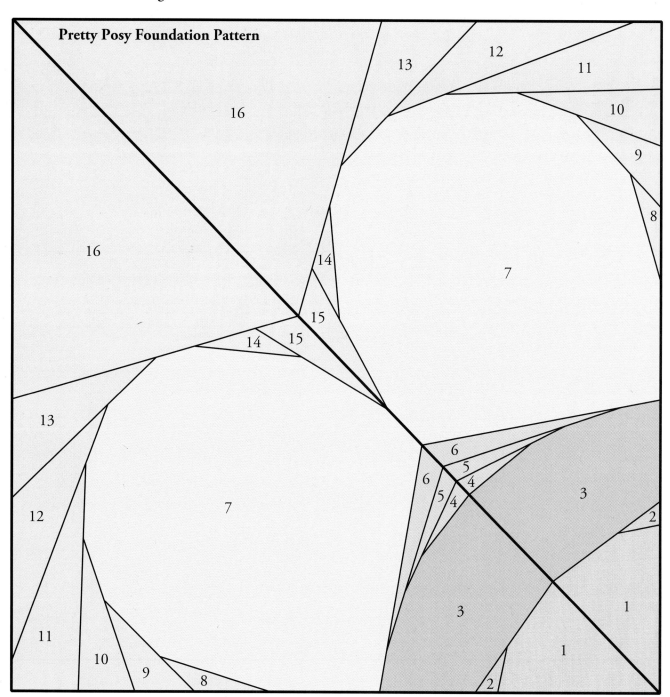

Pretty Posy Foundation Pattern

7. Place Flower Center in center of Petals, covering raw edges of Petals, **Fig 17**. Pin in place.

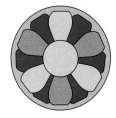

Fig 17

8. Sew along outer edge of circle using a machine zigzag with matching or invisible thread. *Hint: Keep pins in until pillow is sewn together to keep petals out of the way.*

9. Refer to Pillows With Trimmed Edges, page 12, to finish pillow.

Posy Parade

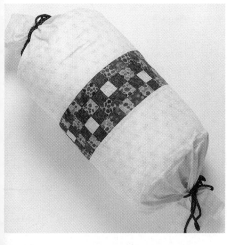

Pillow Size: 14" x 9" neck roll
Technique: Rotary Cutting, page 4

Materials
Fat quarters, med green, dk green, burgundy, yellow
¾ yd lt background
2 yds ribbon or cording
9" x 14" neck-roll pillow form

Cutting
1 – 1½"-wide strip, yellow
2 – 1½"-wide strips, dk green
4 – 1½"-wide strips, burgundy
5 – 1½"-wide strips, med green
2 – 6" x 27½" strips, lt background
2 – 12½" x 27½" strips, lt background

Instructions

1. For rows 1 and 3, sew strips in the sequence shown in **Fig 18**. Repeat.

Fig 18

2. For row 2, sew strips in the sequence shown in **Fig 19**.

3. Cut strip sets at 1½" intervals, **Fig 20**.

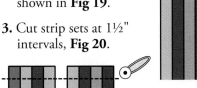

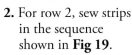

Fig 19

Fig 20

4. Sew rows 1, 2 and 3 together, **Fig 21**, for nine posies.

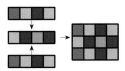

Fig 21

5. Sew posies together turning every other one to form a long strip, **Fig 22**.

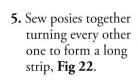

Fig 22

6. Sew 6" x 27½" lt green strip to each side of posy strip; sew 12½" x 27½" lt green strip to each side.

7. Fold posy strip in half crosswise with right sides together; sew along edge opposite fold to form a tube, **Fig 23**.

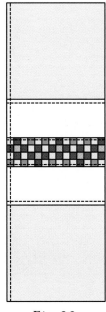

Fig 23

8. For sides, fold under raw edges of tube ¼". Fold again 2½" and sew along first fold, **Fig 24**. Repeat on other side.

9. Turn pillow top right side out; place pillow form inside tube and tie each end with ribbon or cord to finish pillow.

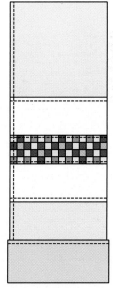

Fig 24

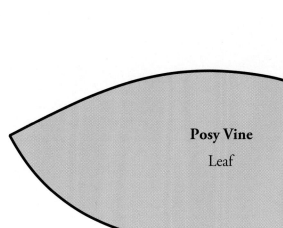

Posy Vine
Leaf

Country Time

This set of charming pillows will give the finishing touch to your country decor.

Hearts

Pillow Size: 14" round
Technique: Easy Machine Appliqué, page 7

Materials

½ yd yellow print (includes backing)
Fat quarters, lt pink, dk pink, green
14" round pillow form
2 yds ruffle trim or make your own
1 yd paper-backed fusible web

Cutting

Note: *Refer to Easy Machine Appliqué to cut out assorted patterns (page 116) from fabric. Use pattern on page 71 for 14½" circles.*

4 – Large Heart, lt pink
4 – Small Heart, dk pink
4 – Leaf, green
1 – Small Circle, green
2 – 14½" Circle, yellow print (pillow front and back)

Instructions

1. Following manufacturer's directions, fuse Hearts, Leaves and Small Circle onto a 14½" Circle, **Fig 1**. Machine-zigzag around edges of flowers, leaves and circle if desired, using matching or invisible thread and small machine zigzag.

Fig 1

2. Refer to Pillows With Trimmed Edges, page 12, or Pillows With Ruffles, page 14, to finish pillow.

Country Basket

Pillow Size: 14" square plus 2"-wide flange
Technique: Easy Machine Appliqué, page 7

Materials

Fat quarters lt pink, med pink, dk pink, green, blue, basket print
Scrap, gold
⅝ yd green print (flange and backing)
14" pillow form
1 yd paper-backed fusible web

Cutting

Note: *Refer to Easy Machine Appliqué to cut out assorted patterns (page 118) from fabric.*

3 Inner Flower, dk pink
3 Middle Flower, med pink
3 Outer Flower, dk pink
3 Flower Center, gold
6 Leaf, green
1 – 6½" x 12½" rectangle, blue
2 – 1½" x 6½" strips, basket print
1 – 1½" x 14½" strip, basket print
1 – 7½" x 14½" rectangle, basket print
2 – 2½" x 14½" strips, green print (flange)
2 – 2½" x 18½" strips, green print (flange)
1 – 18½" square, green print (backing)

Instructions

1. Sew 1½" x 6½" basket print strips to sides of blue rectangle; sew 1½" x 14½" basket print strip to top edge to complete basket handle, **Fig 2**.

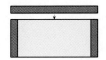

Fig 2

2. Sew basket handle to 7½" x 14½" basket print rectangle, **Fig 3**.

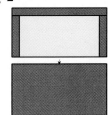

Fig 3

3. Following manufacturer's directions, fuse flowers and leaves to basket referring to photograph and **Fig 4**. Machine-zigzag around edges of flowers and leaves, if desired, using matching or invisible thread and small machine zigzag.

Fig 4

4. Sew 2½" x 14½" green print strips to sides of basket; sew 2½" x 18½" green print strips to top and bottom, **Fig 5**.

Fig 5

5. Refer to Pillows With a Flange, page 13, to finish pillow.

Heart & Tulips

Pillow Size: 12" square
Technique: Easy Machine Appliqué, page 7

Materials

½ yd background
Fat quarters, lt pink, green
Scraps, lt gold, dk gold
12" pillow form
½ yd paper-backed fusible web
1½ yds looped fringe
½ yd paper-backed fusible web

Cutting

Note: *Refer to Easy Machine Appliqué to cut out assorted patterns (page 118) from fabric.*

2 Inner Tulip, dk gold
2 Outer Tulip, lt gold
2 Leaf, green
6 Circles, green
1 Heart, pink
2 – ¼"-wide strips, green (stems)

Instructions

1. Following manufacturer's directions, fuse Tulips, Leaves, Stem and Heart to background referring to photograph and **Fig 6**. Machine-zigzag around edges of flowers and leaves, if desired, using matching or invisible thread and small machine zigzag.

Fig 6

2. Refer to Pillows With Trimmed Edges, page 12, to finish pillow.

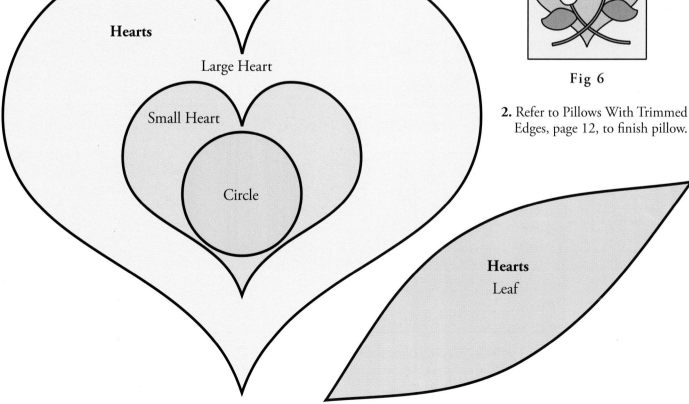

Hearts

Large Heart

Small Heart

Circle

Hearts
Leaf

Lovebirds

Pillow Size: 14" square plus 2"-wide flange

Technique: Easy Machine Appliqué, page 7

Materials

⅝ yd med blue (includes backing)
Fat quarter, lt blue
10" squares, lt gold, dk gold, green, brown, lt pink, dk pink
Scrap, rust
Permanent marking pen, black
1 yd paper-backed fusible web
14" pillow form

Cutting

Note: *Refer to Easy Machine Appliqué to cut out assorted patterns (page 119) from fabric.*

2 – Bird, lt gold (one is flopped)
2 – Wing, dk gold (one is flopped)
2 – Beak, rust
2 – Branch, brown (one is flopped)
6 – Leaf, green
2 – Circle, med blue
1 – Finishing, med blue
1 – Large Heart, lt pink
1 – Small Heart, dk pink
1 – 14½" square, lt blue
2 – 2½" x 14½" strips, med blue (flange)
2 – 2½" x 18½" strips, med blue (flange)
1 – 18½" square, med blue (backing)

Instructions

1. Following manufacturer's directions, fuse Birds, Hearts, Branches, Leaves, Circles and Finishing to background referring to photograph and **Fig 7.** Machine-zigzag around edges of shapes, if desired, using matching or invisible thread and small machine zigzag. Color in birds' eyes with black marking pen.

Fig 7

2. Sew 2½" x 14½" med blue strips to sides of pillow top; sew 2½" x 18½" med blue strips to top and bottom, **Fig 8.**

3. Refer to Pillows With a Flange, page 13, to finish pillow.

Fig 8

Country Posies

Pillow Size: 16" square

Technique: Easy Machine Appliqué, page 7

Materials

Fat quarters lt background, lt green, med green, pink
Scraps, lt gold, med gold
½ yd floral print (border and backing)
16" pillow form
1 yd paper-backed fusible web

Cutting

Note: *Refer to Easy Machine Appliqué to cut out assorted patterns (page 118) from fabric.*

3 – Large Flower, pink
3 – Small Flower, lt gold
3 – Center, dk gold
7 – Leaf, lt green
¼"-wide bias strip, med green
1 – 12½" square, lt background
2 – 2½" x 12½" strips, floral print
2 – 2½" x 16½" strips, floral print
1 – 16½" square, floral print (backing)

Instructions

1. Following manufacturer's directions, fuse Flowers, Leaves and Stems to background square referring to photograph and **Fig 9.** Machine-zigzag around edges of Flowers, Leaves and Stem, if desired, using matching or invisible thread and small machine zigzag.

Fig 9

2. Sew 2½" x 12½" floral print strips to sides of pillow top; sew 2½" x 16½" floral print strips to top and bottom, **Fig 10.**

Fig 10

3. Refer to Basic Pillow, page 12, to finish pillow.

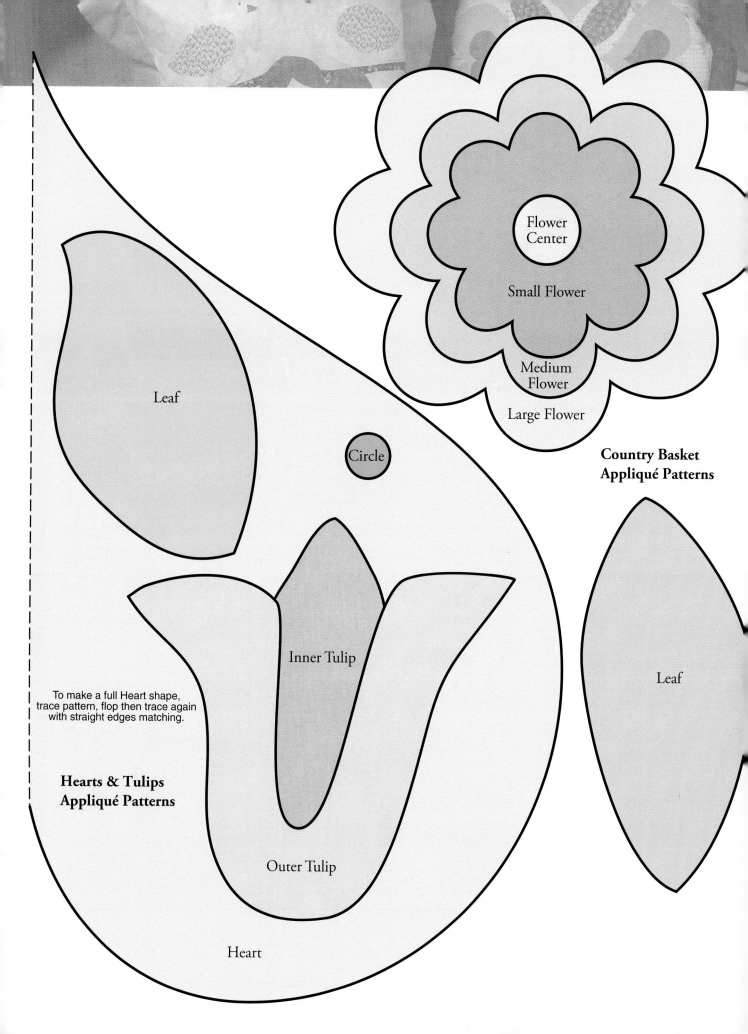

Flower Center

Small Flower

Medium Flower

Large Flower

Country Basket Appliqué Patterns

Leaf

Circle

Leaf

Inner Tulip

To make a full Heart shape, trace pattern, flop then trace again with straight edges matching.

Hearts & Tulips Appliqué Patterns

Outer Tulip

Heart

Leaf

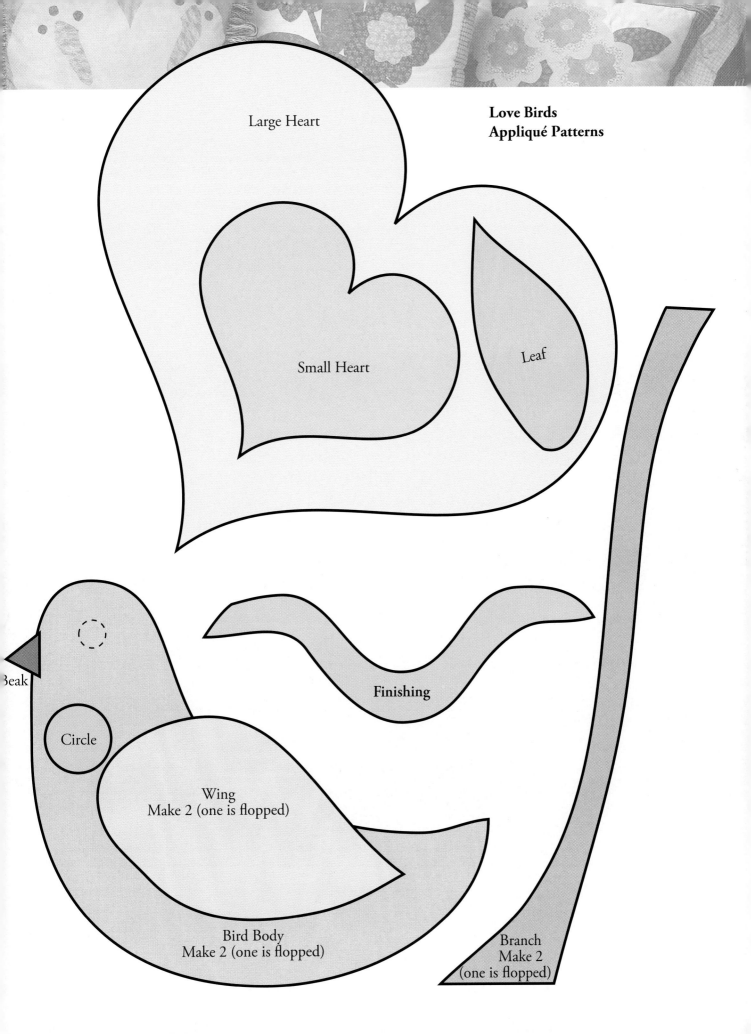

Large Heart

**Love Birds
Appliqué Patterns**

Small Heart

Leaf

Finishing

Beak

Circle

Wing
Make 2 (one is flopped)

Bird Body
Make 2 (one is flopped)

Branch
Make 2
(one is flopped)

Victorian Fancy

Bring the Victorian era to your bedroom or living room with these pillows of crazy quilts, roses, laces, trims and buttons.

Rose

Pillow Size: 14" square
Technique: Foundation Piecing, pages 8 to 11

Materials

Scraps in shades of pink and green (use fabrics with different textures such as satin, velvet, cotton, brocade)
Fat quarter, burgundy
½ yd green (border and backing)
14" pillow form
2 yds beaded trim

Cutting

Note: Foundation piecing does not require exact cutting of pieces.

2 – 2" x 7½" strips, burgundy (first border)
2 – 2" x 10½" strips, burgundy (first border)
2 – 2½" x 10½" strips, green (second border)
2 – 2½" x 14½" strips, green (second border)
1 – 14½" square, green (backing)

Instructions

1. Referring to Foundation Piecing, make one Rose block using pattern on page 122, **Fig 1**.

Fig 1

2. Sew 2" x 7½" burgundy strips to opposite sides of block; sew 2" x 10½" burgundy strips to top and bottom, **Fig 2**.

Fig 2

3. Sew 2½" x 10½" green strips to opposite sides of block; sew 2½" x 14½" green strips to top and bottom to complete pillow top, **Fig 3**.

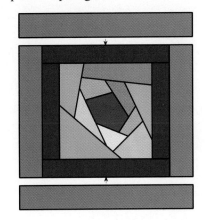

Fig 3

4. Remove paper foundation.

5. Refer to Pillows With Trimmed Edges, page 12, to finish pillow.

Bordered Rose

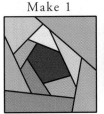

Pillow Size: 14" square
Technique: Foundation Piecing, pages 8 to 11

Materials

Assorted fat quarters and scraps in shades of pink, burgundy and green
14" pillow form

Cutting

Note: Foundation piecing does not require cutting exact pieces.

1 – 14½" square, backing

Instructions

1. Referring to Foundation Piecing, make one large block and 12 small blocks using patterns on pages 122 and 123, **Fig 4**.

Make 1

Make 12

Fig 4

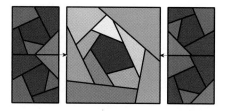

2. Sew small blocks together in pairs, turning them so they aren't all in same direction, then sew a pair to each side of large block, **Fig 5**.

3. Sew two pairs of small blocks together; repeat for another strip. Sew to top and bottom to complete pillow top, **Fig 6**.

4. Remove paper foundations.

5. Refer to Basic Pillow, page 12, to finish pillow.

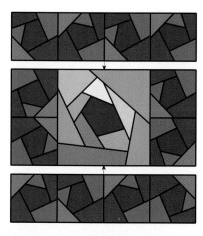

Fig 6

Fig 5

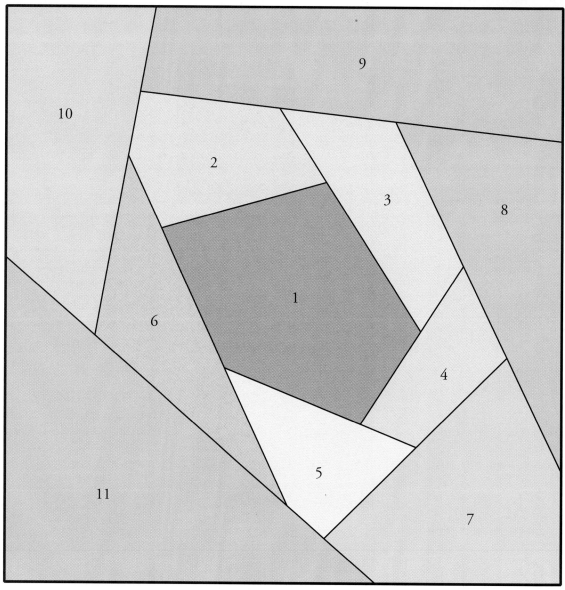

Rose Bordered and Crazy Quilt Foundation Pattern

Crazy Quilt

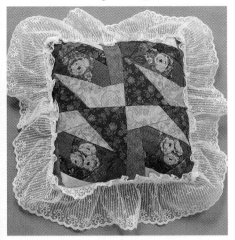

Pillow Size: 12" square
Technique: Foundation Piecing, pages 8 to 11

Materials

Scraps in assorted colors and textures
½ yd black (includes backing)
12" pillow form
2 yds 4"-wide ruffled lace

Cutting

Note: *Foundation piecing does not require exact cutting of pieces.*

1 – 12½" square, backing

Instructions

1. Referring to Foundation Piecing, make four Crazy Quilt blocks using pattern on page 122, **Fig 7**.

Make 4

Fig 7

2. Sew blocks together in pairs then sew pairs together, rotating blocks so they are turned in different directions, **Fig 8**.

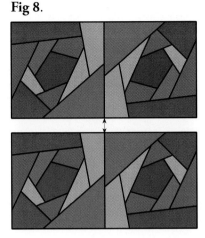

Fig 8

3. Refer to Pillows With Trimmed Edges, page 12, to finish pillow. **Note:** *In photographed model, ruffled lace was added by hand after pillow was finished.*

Rounded Crazy

Pillow Size: 12" round
Technique: Foundation Piecing, pages 8 to 11

Materials

Scraps in assorted colors and textures
Fat quarter, backing
1½ yds cording
12" round pillow form

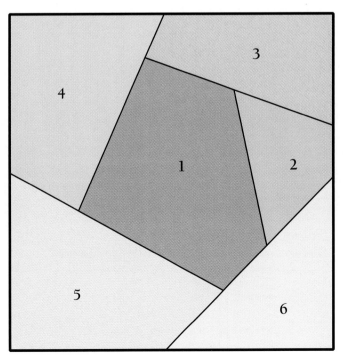

Bordered Rose Foundation Pattern—Border

Cutting

Note: *Foundation piecing does not require cutting exact pieces. Use pattern below to make backing.*

1 – 12½" Circle, backing

Instructions

1. Referring to Foundation Piecing, make four quarter-circle Rounded Crazy blocks using pattern below, **Fig 9.**

Make 4

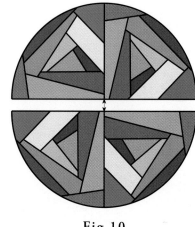

Fig 9

2. Sew blocks together in pairs, then sew pairs together, **Fig 10.**

Fig 10

3. Remove paper foundations.

4. Refer to Pillows With Trimmed Edges, page 12, to finish pillow.

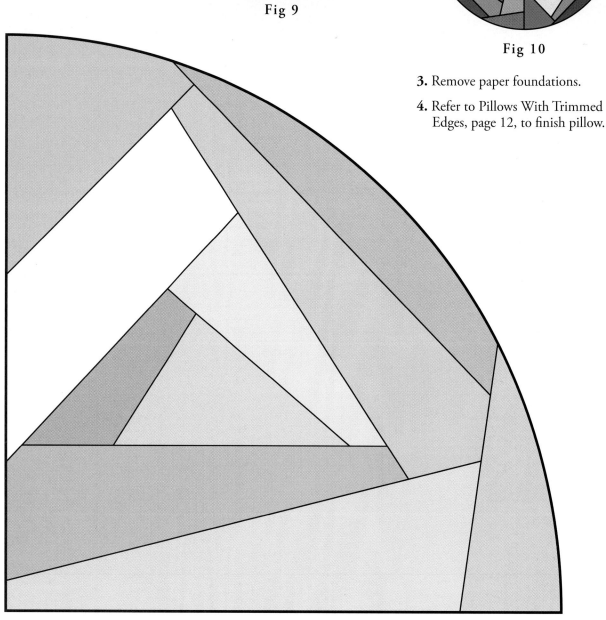

Rounded Crazy Foundation Pattern

Mysterious

Pillow Size: 14" square

Technique: Foundation Piecing, pages 8 to 11.

Materials

Scraps in assorted colors and textures
½ yd tulle or see-through lacy material
Fat quarter, backing
Eight ribbon roses
½ yd ¼"-wide satin ribbon
14" square pillow form

Cutting

Note: Foundation piecing does not require exact cutting of pieces.

1 – 14½" square, backing

Instructions

1. Referring to Foundation Piecing, make four Mysterious blocks using pattern on page 126, **Fig 11**.

Make 4

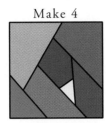

Fig 11

2. Sew blocks together in pairs, then sew pairs together, rotating blocks so they aren't in same direction, **Fig 12**.

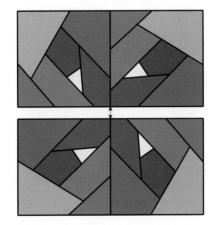

Fig 12

3. Remove paper foundations.

4. Cut lace or tulle so it is 15½" long by the width of fabric. Fold each long raw edge under ¼", then another ¼"; sew along first fold. Sew two rows of long basting stitches along each long edge. Sew first row about ⅛" from edge and second row ¼" from edge, **Fig 13**.

Fig 13

5. Pull basting stitches so lace now measures 14½" x 14½", then baste gathered edges of lace to pillow top. Pinch lace together in center and tie loosely with a string to keep out of the way, **Fig 14**.

Fig 14

6. Refer to Basic Pillow, page 12, to finish pillow.

7. Referring to photograph, wrap ribbon around lace, then tack down center with large ribbon roses.

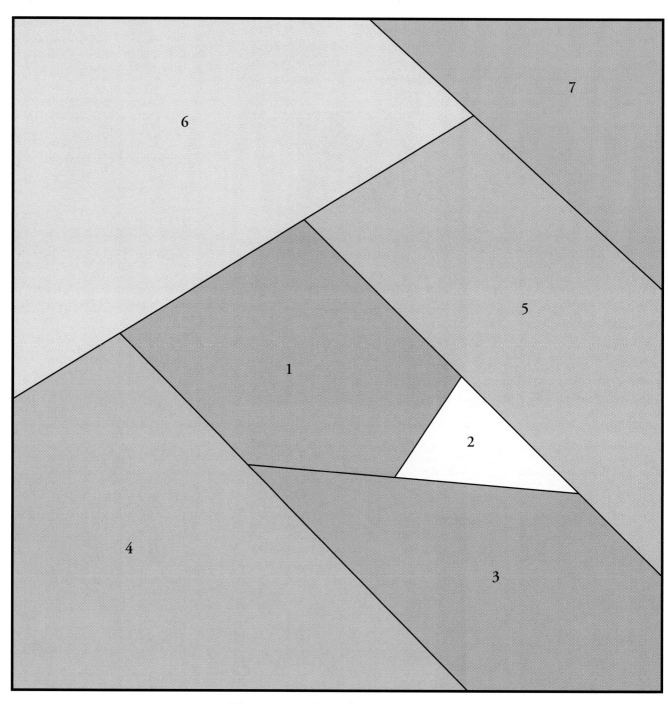

Mysterious Foundation Pattern

Glory Rose

Pillow Size: 12" x 16" rectangle
Technique: Foundation Piecing, pages
8 to 11

Materials

Fat quarters, med pink, lt pink, dk pink
½ yd green (includes border and
  backing)
2 yds fringe
12" x 16" pillow form

Cutting

*Note: Foundation piecing does not require
exact cutting of pieces.*

2 – 1¼" x 8" strips, blue
2 – 1¼" x 8" strips, dk pink
2 – 1¼" x 13½" strips, dk pink
2 – 2" x 9½" strips, green
2 – 2" x 16½" strips, green

Instructions

1. Referring to Foundation Piecing,
make Glory Rose block using pattern
on page 128, **Fig 15**.

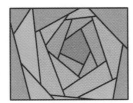

Fig 15

2. Sew 1¼" x 8" blue strips to sides of
block, **Fig 16**.

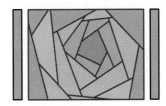

Fig 16

3. Sew 1¼" x 8" dk pink strips to sides
of block; sew 1¼" x 13½" dk pink
strips to top and bottom, **Fig 17**.

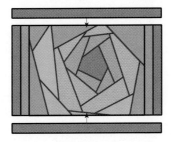

Fig 17

4. Sew 2" x 9½" green strips to sides of
block; sew 2" x 16½" green strips to
top and bottom to complete pillow
top, **Fig 18**.

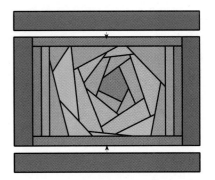

Fig 18

5. Remove paper foundations.

6. Refer to Pillows With Trimmed
Edges, page 12, to finish pillow.

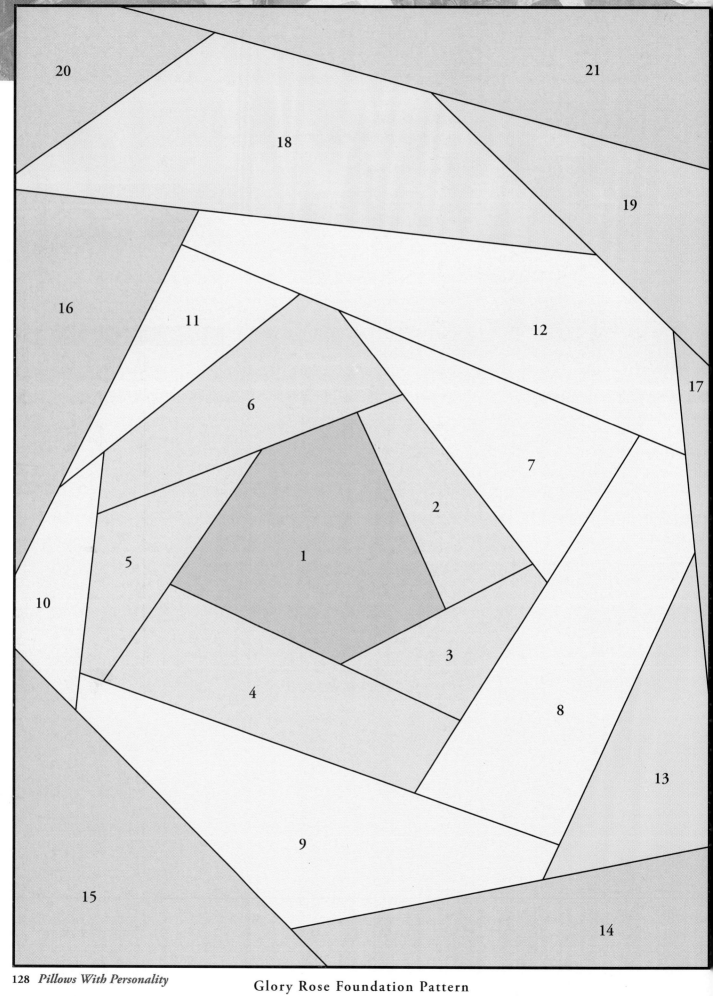

Glory Rose Foundation Pattern